# CULLODEN 1746

▼'The Battle of Culloden'
engraved by Laurie and
Whittle, published in May
1747. This is one of the
most famous of the
contemporary engravings
of the battle and is typical
of the period, with the
emphasis on the victorious
general. Various events in
the battle are depicted
including the Campbells
breaking down the walls,
the close combat on the
left of the Royal line, and
the cavalry movement on
the Jacobite left. However,
the overall impression is
incorrect, particularly the
position of Cumberland
and his staff. (Anne S. K.
Brown Military Collection,
Brown University)

# CULLODEN 1746

## PETER HARRINGTON

*This book is dedicated to the dead – both English and*
*Scottish – who lie below Culloden's turf*

First published in Great Britain in
1991 by Osprey Publishing,
Elms Court, Chapel Way, Botley,
Oxford OX2 9LP, UK.

Email: info@ospreypublishing.com

© Copyright 1991
Osprey Publishing Ltd.
00 01 02 03 04  10 9 8 7 6 5 4 3 2 1

Also published as Campaign 12
*Culloden 1746*

Produced by DAG Publications Ltd
for Osprey Publishing Ltd. Colour
bird's eye view illustrations by Cilla
Eurich. Cartography by Micromap.
Tourist Information by Martin Marix
Evans. Back cover Cartography by The
Map Studio. Typeset by Ronset
Typesetters, Darwen, Lancashire.
Mono camerawork by M&E
Reproductions, North Fambridge,
Printed in China through World Print
Ltd.

*British Library Cataloguing in*
*Publication Data*
Harrington, Peter *1954–*
Culloden 1746. – (Osprey campaign
series, v. 12).
1. Scotland. Wars, history, 1714–
1820
I. Title
941.072
ISBN 1 84176 187 7

FRONT COVER: The Battle of
Culloden © Mark Churms
2000/thehistoryweb.com

# CONTENTS

▲ *Another contemporary scene of Culloden, published a month after the battle. Many of the incidents are more or less correctly identified, but give a confusing impression. Cumberland is close by Kingston's Horse who are galloping on to the flank of the Jacobites. The position of the Royal ranks is correct although Wolfe's Regiment is still in line. On the extreme left, Kerr's and Cobham's dragoons are passing between the broken walls.* (Tradition *Magazine*)

FOR A CATALOGUE OF ALL BOOKS PUBLISHED BY OSPREY MILITARY, AUTOMOTIVE AND AVIATION PLEASE WRITE TO:

The Marketing Manager, Osprey Direct UK, PO Box 140, Wellingborough, Northants, NN8 4ZA, United Kingdom.
Email: info@ospreydirect.co.uk

The Marketing Manager, Osprey Direct USA, PO Box 130, Sterling Heights, MI 48311-0130, USA.
Email: info@ospreydirectusa.com

VISIT OSPREY AT
www.ospreypublishing.com

# The March of the Jacobite Army, 1745

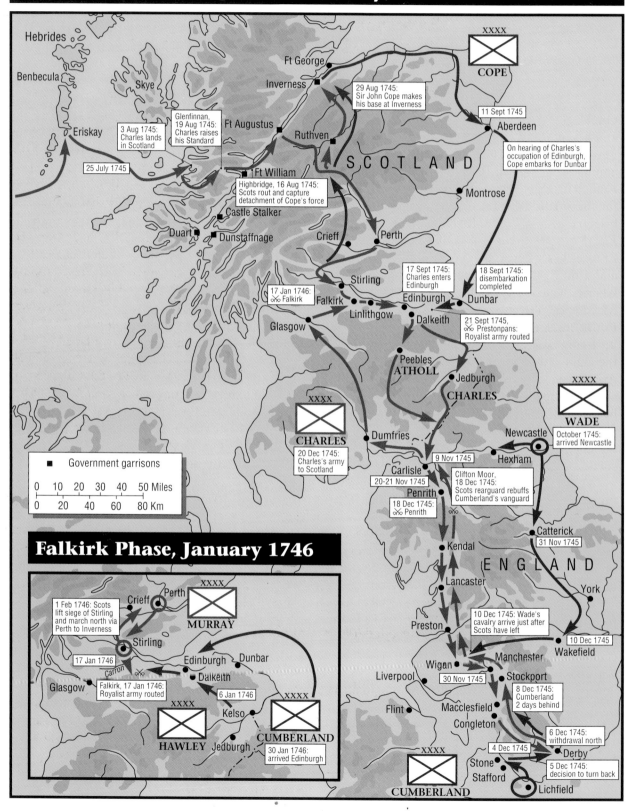

Hebrides

Benbecula

Skye

Ft George

Inverness

COPE

29 Aug 1745: Sir John Cope makes his base at Inverness

11 Sept 1745

Aberdeen

On hearing of Charles's occupation of Edinburgh, Cope embarks for Dunbar

Eriskay

3 Aug 1745: Charles lands in Scotland

Glenfinnan, 19 Aug 1745: Charles raises his Standard

Ft Augustus

Ruthven

25 July 1745

SCOTLAND

Montrose

Ft William

Highbridge, 16 Aug 1745: Scots rout and capture detachment of Cope's force

Castle Stalker

Duart

Dunstaffnage

Crieff

Perth

17 Sept 1745: Charles enters Edinburgh

18 Sept 1745: disembarkation completed

Stirling

17 Jan 1746: ✂ Falkirk

Falkirk

Edinburgh

Dunbar

Linlithgow

Dalkeith

21 Sept 1745, ✂ Prestonpans: Royalist army routed

Glasgow

Peebles

ATHOLL

Jedburgh

CHARLES

WADE

October 1745: arrived Newcastle

CHARLES

20 Dec 1745: Charles's army to Scotland

Dumfries

Newcastle

9 Nov 1745

Hexham

Carlisle

20-21 Nov 1745

Clifton Moor, 18 Dec 1745: Scots rearguard rebuffs Cumberland's vanguard

18 Dec 1745: ✂ Penrith

Penrith

Catterick

31 Nov 1745

- Government garrisons

0  10  20  30  40  50 Miles

0  20  40  60  80 Km

Kendal

ENGLAND

Lancaster

York

10 Dec 1745: Wade's cavalry arrive just after Scots have left

## Falkirk Phase, January 1746

Preston

10 Dec 1745

Wakefield

Crieff

Perth

MURRAY

1 Feb 1746: Scots lift siege of Stirling and march north via Perth to Inverness

Stirling

Wigan

Manchester

Liverpool

30 Nov 1745

Stockport

17 Jan 1746

Carron

Edinburgh

Dunbar

Dalkeith

8 Dec 1745: Cumberland 2 days behind

Falkirk, 17 Jan 1746: Royalist army routed

Glasgow

6 Jan 1746

Kelso

CUMBERLAND

HAWLEY

Jedburgh

30 Jan 1746: arrived Edinburgh

Flint

Macclesfield

Congleton

6 Dec 1745: withdrawal north

4 Dec 1745

Derby

CUMBERLAND

Stone

Stafford

5 Dec 1745: decision to turn back

Lichfield

# BACKGROUND TO THE 'FORTY-FIVE'

On 16 July 1745, Prince Charles Edward Stuart and a handful of supporters, known as the 'Seven Men of Moidart', with a small quantity of arms and ammunition, set sail from Brest aboard two small French frigates, *Du Teillay* and *Elizabeth*, bound for the small Hebridean island of Eriskay. After a brief run-in with the Royal Navy's HMS *Lion*, *Elizabeth* was damaged and had to return to France. With her went most of the military stores and a number of French volunteers. Undeterred, Charles landed on Eriskay, to be met by Alexander Macdonald of Boisdale who advised him to return to the continent. The Prince would have none of it; 'I am come home, sir,' he replied. He reached the mainland of Scotland, at Loch nan Uamh near Arisaig, on 25 July and three weeks later, having solicited support from among the Highland chiefs, he raised his standard at Glenfinnan on 19 August, at which time his father was proclaimed James VIII of Scotland and III of England, and the Prince, his successor.

The 1,200 men who were present at Glenfinnan saw Charles as the rightful heir to the thrones of England and Scotland. It had been more than fifty years since a Stuart had ruled Great Britain, but since the 'Glorious Revolution' of 1688 both countries had been led by Protestant claimants from the continent, beginning with William of Orange and his wife Mary. Being forced to flee, James II found sanctuary in France, and an enthusiastic supporter in Louis XIV, the old enemy of William, who saw in his English fugitive an opportunity to gain revenge for his defeats at the hands of the Dutchman. In Britain James's followers, known as Jacobites from the Latin name for James, planned to restore their rightful leader and it was left to John Graham of Claverhouse, Viscount Dundee, to lead a revolt in 1689, but his death following the successful victory over English troops at the Pass of Killiecrankie on 27 July left the Jacobite cause leaderless. James was forced to remain in exile where he died in 1701. His son was proclaimed King James VIII of Scotland and III of England in absentia. The 13-year-old was now the claimant, or pretender, to the throne, but the 'Old Pretender' had to wait his chance.

It was not all woe for the Jacobites, however. In 1702 William died, having been thrown from his horse, to be succeeded by James's younger daughter Anne, sister to Mary. William had been unpopular among Catholics in both kingdoms, particularly in the Scottish Highlands. Yet for six years James and his supporters dallied – while making plans for a military confrontation. Finally, with 6,000 French troops aboard thirty vessels, the 'Old Pretender' sailed, but was forced to return to Dunkirk by the Royal Navy. It was to be another seven years before the next enterprise, this time led by James's confederate in Scotland, the Earl of Mar, who raised the Royal Standard at Braemar in September 1715, thereby initiating what popularly became known as the 'Fifteen' Rebellion. This was better planned than previous attempts and the Jacobite forces – 10,000 men – actually brought the army of the new English king, George I, to battle. Sheriffmuir, fought on 13 November 1715, proved inconclusive, however, and the Jacobites were forced to retreat. On the previous day at Preston in northern England the Jacobites had gained a tactical victory, but failed to follow it up due to confusion and dissent among the various leaders. Unaware of the outcome, James himself had landed in Aberdeenshire, but was forced – together with the disillusioned Mar – to re-embark in February 1716 for France, where the Pretender would spend the rest of his days. A brief and feeble attempt at another adventure, this time with Spanish help, came to grief in the Pass of Glenshiel in June 1719, where Jacobite and

▲'Battle of Glenshiel', 1719' by Lionel Edwards. At the urging of the Jacobite Duke of Ormonde, the Spanish set out to invade England. Despite losing many of their ships in a storm, 300 Spanish troops landed and joined up with 1,500 Highlanders but were routed at Glenshiel by 1,100 Royal troops under General Wightman thus ending another Jacobite uprising. (Anne S. K. Brown Military Collection, Brown University)

▲ James Francis Edward Stuart, the Old Pretender (1688-1766) as Prince of Wales in 1705. On the death of Queen Anne the Elector of Hanover was proclaimed king. James, the son of James II, was convinced that he should regain the throne as rightful heir and had himself proclaimed King James VIII of Scotland and III of England at Braemar on 25 September 1715. With a small army under the Earl of Mar, the Jacobites confronted the king's supporters at Sherrifmuir but the battle was inconclusive and the rising soon collapsed. (Anne S. K. Brown Military Collection, Brown University)

Spanish soldiers were no match for the English troops from the garrison at Inverness. Acutely aware of the Jacobite intentions in Scotland to stage a *coup*, and determined to subdue any uprising, the government at Westminster ordered Field Marshal George Wade to establish a chain of strategically sited forts that were linked by military roads.

For twenty-five years the English garrisons policed the Highlands successfully. Unbeknown to them, however, were the various schemes being hatched for a new attempt to overthrow the King. The Westminster government was already embroiled in a war with Spain when, in 1743, the French developed plans for an invasion which would link up with a Jacobite force assembled in the western Highlands. A second force under Marshal Saxe and Prince Charles Edward was to land on the south coast of England within striking distance of London, but many of the French transports were wrecked or badly damaged by a gale which hit the French fleet off Brest in March 1744. It had been a half-hearted escapade by the French and the disaster gave them a suitable excuse to withdraw from the venture leaving Charles without his major ally. Undaunted, he decided that the rebellion must come from within and instructed his supporters in Scotland to make plans for his arrival in June 1745. They did not share the Prince's optimism, and feared that the loss of French assistance would doom any uprising from the start.

▲'General George Wade'(1673-1748) by Van Diest. The future field marshal visited Scotland in 1724 to reconnoitre the strength and resources of the Jacobites. Shortly afterwards, he became commander of His Majesty's Forces in Scotland and superintended the construction of military roads and bridges. He was popular despite having had to disarm the Highlands. The work was commenced in 1726 using 500 soldiers and was well advanced by 1729. In the 1730s he became governor of the newly built forts of the Great Glen and during the rising commanded the Royal army at Newcastle. (Anne S. K. Brown Military Collection, Brown University)

▶'George II' (1683-1760) by Pine. At Dettingen, George directed the victorious British forces. Three years later his second son, the Duke of Cumberland, commanded the army at Culloden. When the Jacobites reached Derby the king had his yachts crammed with the most precious of his possessions and ready to sail from Tower Quay at short notice. Hearing of the victory at Culloden he asked about his son and was reassured of his safety. (Anne S. K. Brown Military Collection, Brown University)

## Opening Movements

Letters and appeals dissuading the Prince from his scheme fell on deaf ears and he duly landed in July. The events at Glenfinnan stirred many men who began to feel that the rising might be possible after all. The nucleus of the Jacobite army numbered about 1, 300 men, none of whom, with the exception of one or two officers, had ever experienced military service let alone warfare. Fortunately for them, the Government could bring little to bear against this raw force as it had let the strengths of the garrisons fall short of the original numbers, and could only muster about 3, 000 men, including invalids who were garrisoning several castles. Sir John Cope had the unenviable task of commanding this weak force and putting down the rebellion. He should have concentrated his force

▶*Trooper of the 13th Dragoons, circa 1742. At Prestonpans the regiment was commanded by Colonel James Gardiner, who was slain in the battle. Thereafter the 13th Dragoons saw action at Falkirk, where it charged in a blinding storm of rain and wind. The regiment did not see action at Culloden but was employed in patrolling the roads around Edinburgh. (Anne S. K. Brown Military Collection, Brown University)*

at Stirling protected by the Firth of Forth, but instead he was advised by his superiors to make his base at Fort Augustus. Intelligence on the movements of Charles and rumours of a French invasion, however, led Cope to alter his plans and he moved to Inverness on 29 August.

The Highland army was allowed free range across central Scotland and they took advantage of Cope's absence to attack the Government depot at Ruthven. Actually, the first contact between the two sides occurred earlier, on 16 August when two companies of recruits of the Royal Scots, stationed at Perth, moved to strengthen Fort William. At Highbridge, spanning the River Spean on the road from Fort William to Fort Augustus, Macdonald of Tiendrish, with a dozen men and a piper, drove the Royal troops into retreat without a fight. The Highlanders captured the small force shortly afterwards. The main part of the Jacobite army moved towards Edinburgh and occupied the Scottish capital.

### The Battle of Prestonpans

When Cope received this news he embarked his troops at Aberdeen and landed at Dunbar. The Highlanders moved out to meet them and on 21 September the two armies came face to face. Cope was satisfied with the terrain: 'There is not in the whole of the ground between Edinburgh and Dunbar, a better Spot for both Horse and Foot to act upon,' he said. With his position behind a marsh and ditch with the sea to his rear and dragoon regiments upon each flank, with infantry

▼'Battle of Prestonpans', 1745, by Sir William Allan. After capturing Edinburgh the Highland army moved eastwards and encountered Sir John Cope with 3,000 troops near Preston House. As soon as the clansmen charged, the king's artillerymen took to their heels followed by the dragoons and, finally, the infantry. In this Victorian recreation, a Highlander swings his axe to fell Colonel Gardiner while the Prince and Murray watch the battle. (Anne S. K. Brown Military Collection, Brown University)

▶Charles Edward Stuart (1720-88) after a picture by Robert Strange drawn at Edinburgh in 1745. After Culloden, Charles fled to France, but in 1750 he came to London in disguise and met leading Jacobites. He also reconnoitred the approaches to the Tower of London. It was in London also that the Prince converted temporarily to Protestantism, a move that might have had dramatic consequences five years earlier. (Anne S. K. Brown Military Collection, Brown University)

# The Battle of Prestonpans, 21 September 1745

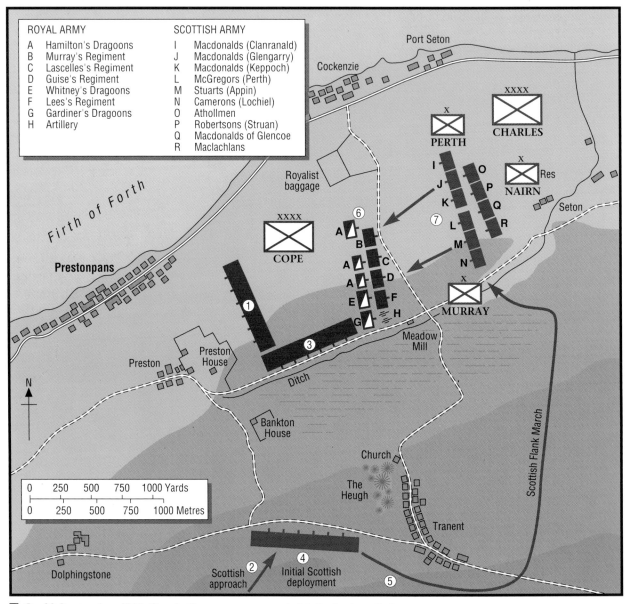

ROYAL ARMY
A   Hamilton's Dragoons
B   Murray's Regiment
C   Lascelles's Regiment
D   Guise's Regiment
E   Whitney's Dragoons
F   Lees's Regiment
G   Gardiner's Dragoons
H   Artillery

SCOTTISH ARMY
I   Macdonalds (Clanranald)
J   Macdonalds (Glengarry)
K   Macdonalds (Keppoch)
L   McGregors (Perth)
M   Stuarts (Appin)
N   Camerons (Lochiel)
O   Athollmen
P   Robertsons (Struan)
Q   Macdonalds of Glencoe
R   Maclachlans

**1** On 20 September 1745, Cope's Government army initially deploys facing west, expecting the Jacobites to approach from the direction of Edinburgh.

**2** The Jacobite army, led by Lord George Murray, approaches from a more southerly direction than anticipated by Cope.

**3** The Government army redeploys facing south.

**4** The Jacobite deploy, but reconnaissance indicates that an attack across the marsh and ditch (albeit downhill) in front of Cope's army would be impracticable.

**5** Disagreement over what to do next leads the Jacobites to send a detachment west and then recall it; and finally the decision is taken to continue to the right and attack Cope from the east.

**6** Several changes of front during the evening and night end with Cope's army turned to meet an attack from the new position taken up by the Jacobites.

**7** At dawn the Jacobites attack.

in the middle, Cope waited for the enemy to make their move. After various flanking movements both sides found that their left wings were outflanked by their opponents' right. Soon both wings of the Prince's army, 2,500 men massed in dense columns, moved towards the Royal lines. The charging Highlanders to the front and right were too much for the Government artillerymen who quickly took to their heels. The Royal dragoons were similarly ineffective and the infantry only managed to fire one volley before they too ran away. Cope tried in vain to rally his men, but was forced to flee at the head of four hundred stragglers to Berwick-on-Tweed, leaving behind 500 dead, more than 1,000 prisoners and many wounded. His victory, achieved in just over five minutes, so impressed Charles that he began to consider his army invincible. The French too began to pay closer attention, feeling perhaps that the Prince might be able to do their work for them.

Upon news of the defeat the Government recalled ten battalions from Flanders and began to recruit more men. This was a popular move throughout England and loyal associations sprang up, offering men and money to thwart any Jacobite incursions. Scotland was now virtually under the control of Prince Charles save for a few outlying garrisons holed-up in the castles at Edinburgh, Dunbarton and Stirling. The English marchlands prepared for an emergency and the inhabitants of Carlisle assumed a defensive posture and began to build breastworks, but the place was still highly vulnerable. On 9 November, Charles's clansmen appeared before the city.

## The Invasion of England

Refusing entry to the Highland army, the guns of Carlisle castle opened up. Hearing a false report of English troops fast approaching, Charles moved his army away but returned shortly after to resume siege operations. This was too much for the citizens who forced Lieutenant-Colonel Durand under protest to move his small garrison of invalid officers into the castle, but faced with the threat from the Prince that the inhabitants would be put to the sword and the town torched if the castle did not surrender, Durand capitulated. Field Marshal Wade's movement from Newcastle in an attempt to relieve Carlisle came to nothing owing to poor weather. Nothing appeared to stand in the way of the Jacobites as they quit Carlisle and moved

▼*Carlisle in an engraving of April 1745. The city walls were in utter disrepair and defended by 80 invalids who, even under the direction of Lieutenant-Colonel Durand, could not prevent the city from falling on 15 November. Five weeks later it was Cumberland's turn to invest the city which fell on 30 December. The Duke's conditions were: 'All the terms his R. Highness will or can grant to the rebel garrison of Carlisle are – That they shall not be put to the sword, but be reserved for the King's pleasure.' (Anne S. K. Brown Military Collection, Brown University)*

southwards in late November 1745, but not until they reached Preston did they encounter any enthusiasm from the local population – although few local men came forward to volunteer. Manchester saw the largest welcome laid at the feet of the Prince. Bonfires were lighted and bells were rung in his honour, but, again, few men came forward to offer their services. Those few that did – mainly unemployed labourers – were formed with other English volunteers by Francis Towneley into the 'Manchester Regiment'.

The absence of any opposition inspired the Pretender to press on. The local militia had failed to make an appearance and General Wade's columns were still moving slowly down through Yorkshire. However, Charles quickly learned that the Duke of Cumberland, the King's son and successor to Lord Ligonier as commander of the main Royal army, was massing his force of 2,000 horse and 8,250 foot in Staffordshire to threaten any movement towards Derby and the London

▲ *'The March of the Guards towards Scotland' by Hogarth. In this famous scene Hogarth has represented soldiers saying farewell to their families, supposedly at the turnpike at Tottenham Court Road before marching to a camp at Finchley to prepare for the threat from the Jacobites. In the middle distance the troops can be seen setting off up the Great North Road. (Anne S. K. Brown Military Collection, Brown University)*

road. The Jacobites made a cunning feint towards Wales and drew Cumberland in that direction, leaving Derby open. On 4 December Charles entered the town but was faced with a dilemma. Cumberland, being so close, would detect the ruse and could soon be at Stafford. In the east Wade was making good time and would soon join up with the new army being formed in London. A total of 30,000 could then be brought to bear against the 5,000 clansmen who were now more than a hundred miles from their homeland.

While Charles and his staff were pondering their next move, the morale in the Jacobite army could not have been higher, but the soldiers were unaware of the decisions being made in the War Council. Lord George Murray was for an immediate retreat, but the Prince wanted to continue the advance towards London. To back his case, he presented news of Lord Drummond's arrival in Scotland with French backing, but many felt that this would be of no use to the Jacobites in England. After much debate Charles reluctantly agreed to a withdrawal back to Scotland. Two days after entering Derby the retreat northwards began. Despite rumours that the army was moving to attack Wade and join with the French troops under Drummond, the clansmen were despondent. They had come so close to achieving their goal and now it was all for naught.

The retreat was followed closely by Cumberland with cavalry and dragoons and he was now within two days of striking the Scots. By the time the Jacobites were into Westmorland their artillery and ammunition wagons had fallen a long way behind. In the rear were Glengarry's men who were joined on the Shap fells by John Roy Stewart. Near the village of Shap, the clansmen were aware of enemy movements. A group of government mounted militia approached but moved off when threatened. At nearby Clifton a brief action took place in the village lanes between Cumberland's dragoons and some of the Jacobite cavalry, followed shortly by an advance of three dismounted dragoon regiments against the Jacobite rearguard. Hand-to-hand fighting broke out and the Royal troops were forced to break off the engagement, allowing the Jacobite retreat to proceed unchecked. Cumberland was forced to halt his exhausted troops in the wintery weather that was sweeping down over the fells. On 20 December, two days after Clifton, the Scottish army crossed into Scotland.

## The Campaign of Falkirk

Safely back in Scotland, Charles's force grew in numbers with the addition of further clans under Lord Strathallan and Drummond's 750 Irish troops in the service of France. The task of dispersing the Jacobite army now fell squarely upon the shoulders of Lieutenant-General Henry Hawley, brought in to replace Cumberland who had been called back to London to prepare the capital for an anticipated French invasion. Edinburgh, Stirling Castle, the Highland forts and Inverness had already been occupied by Royal troops and independent companies during the Jacobite foray into England, and the Scottish capital served as the staging-post for the next phase of offensive operations. The Jacobites were massing at Perth and in January 1746, with the train of artillery which Drummond had brought from France, began the siege of Stirling Castle, despite the fact that the height of the castle above the surrounding land made it virtually impossible to find suitable positions for siting the batteries.

Hawley arrived at Edinburgh on 6 January and began to gather his army of twelve regiments, some having recently landed from Flanders. His Achilles' heel was the artillery, a strange array of weapons taken from Edinburgh castle and manned by a motley band of country artisans. Ten days later, Hawley with his force of 8, 000 men was at Falkirk in an attempt to raise the siege at Stirling. Lord George Murray was aware of this threat and on the previous day had moved the Jacobite army, 9,000 strong, to Plean Moor, two miles from the village of Bannockburn within sight of Stirling Castle where 1,000 Highlanders remained in the trenches. On the 17th the Jacobites moved off in two columns, unbeknown to Hawley who was having breakfast at Callander House with the Countess of Kilmarnock. Not until afternoon did he realize the gravity of the situation after the Jacobites had moved to occupy the hill above Falkirk. He immediately ordered his troops on to the ridge where they arrived as the weather broke. Rain began to soak the opposing forces as they deployed facing one another. The Royal infantry were in two lines of six regiments with the dragoons on the left, and no sooner had the infantry formed up than Hawley sent forward his cavalry against the Jacobite right wing. This was immediately neutralized by a Highland volley which brought down eighty horsemen. This was too much for the survivors who turned their mounts and fled headlong right into their own infantry on the left wing. The torrential rain having soaked the cartridges of their muskets, the clans-

# THE BATTLE OF FALKIRK

## Late afternoon of 17 January 1746

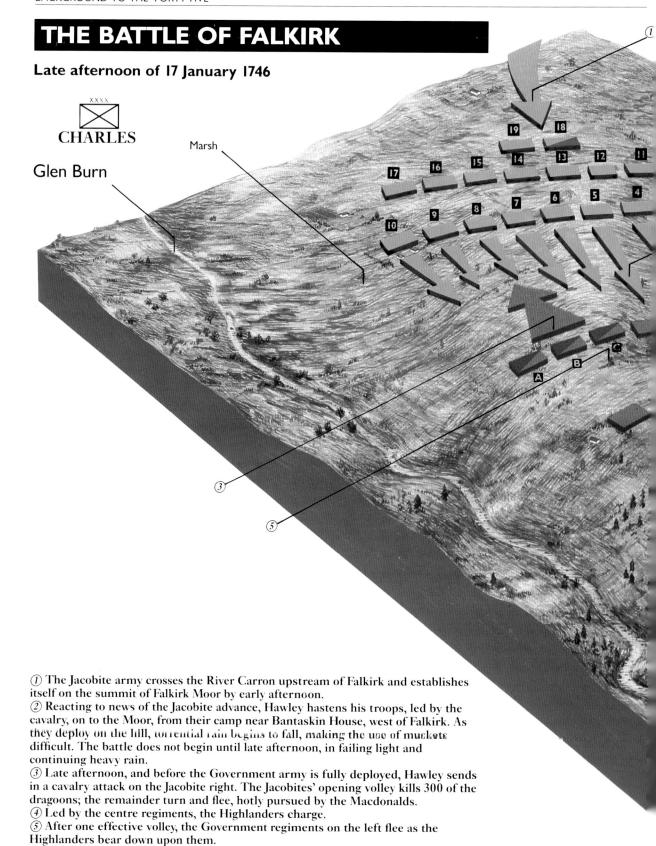

CHARLES

Glen Burn

Marsh

① The Jacobite army crosses the River Carron upstream of Falkirk and establishes itself on the summit of Falkirk Moor by early afternoon.
② Reacting to news of the Jacobite advance, Hawley hastens his troops, led by the cavalry, on to the Moor, from their camp near Bantaskin House, west of Falkirk. As they deploy on the hill, torrential rain begins to fall, making the use of muskets difficult. The battle does not begin until late afternoon, in failing light and continuing heavy rain.
③ Late afternoon, and before the Government army is fully deployed, Hawley sends in a cavalry attack on the Jacobite right. The Jacobites' opening volley kills 300 of the dragoons; the remainder turn and flee, hotly pursued by the Macdonalds.
④ Led by the centre regiments, the Highlanders charge.
⑤ After one effective volley, the Government regiments on the left flee as the Highlanders bear down upon them.

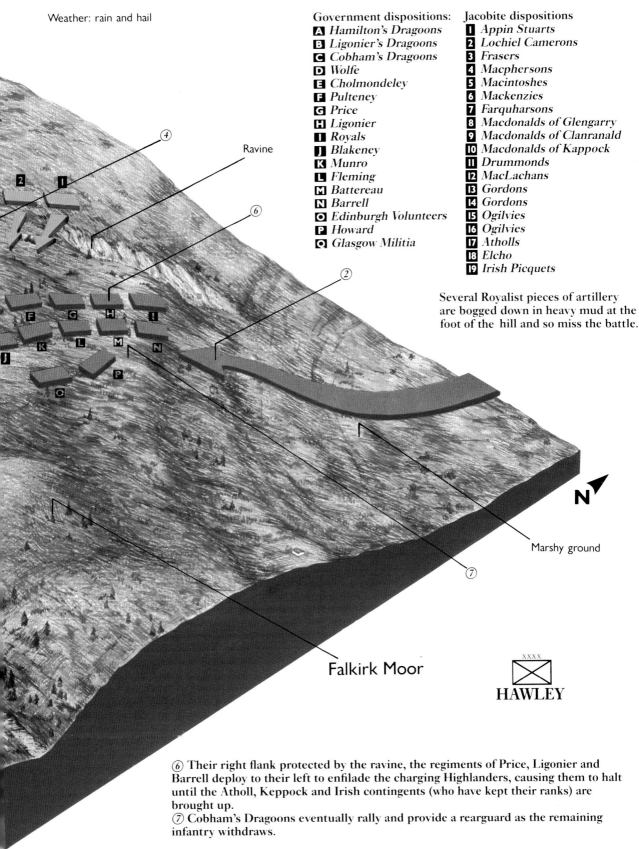

Weather: rain and hail

Government dispositions:

- **A** *Hamilton's Dragoons*
- **B** *Ligonier's Dragoons*
- **C** *Cobham's Dragoons*
- **D** *Wolfe*
- **E** *Cholmondeley*
- **F** *Pulteney*
- **G** *Price*
- **H** *Ligonier*
- **I** *Royals*
- **J** *Blakeney*
- **K** *Munro*
- **L** *Fleming*
- **M** *Battereau*
- **N** *Barrell*
- **O** *Edinburgh Volunteers*
- **P** *Howard*
- **Q** *Glasgow Militia*

Jacobite dispositions

- **1** *Appin Stuarts*
- **2** *Lochiel Camerons*
- **3** *Frasers*
- **4** *Macphersons*
- **5** *Macintoshes*
- **6** *Mackenzies*
- **7** *Farquharsons*
- **8** *Macdonalds of Glengarry*
- **9** *Macdonalds of Clanranald*
- **10** *Macdonalds of Kappock*
- **11** *Drummonds*
- **12** *MacLachans*
- **13** *Gordons*
- **14** *Gordons*
- **15** *Ogilvies*
- **16** *Ogilvies*
- **17** *Atholls*
- **18** *Elcho*
- **19** *Irish Picquets*

Several Royalist pieces of artillery are bogged down in heavy mud at the foot of the hill and so miss the battle.

Ravine

Marshy ground

Falkirk Moor

HAWLEY

⑥ Their right flank protected by the ravine, the regiments of Price, Ligonier and Barrell deploy to their left to enfilade the charging Highlanders, causing them to halt until the Atholl, Keppock and Irish contingents (who have kept their ranks) are brought up.
⑦ Cobham's Dragoons eventually rally and provide a rearguard as the remaining infantry withdraws.

men in the centre charged with their swords. Their opponents fired one haphazard volley and then took to their heels. Had it not been for the enfilading fire from three regiments on the government right, the outcome would have been much worse, but they too were eventually forced to quit the hill in the direction of Linlithgow. Three guns from Hawley's artillery, which had been stuck in a bog and saw no part in the action, were salvaged but the other guns fell into the hands of the Jacobites. A total of 300 Royal troops were captured and a further 350 lay dying on the rain-soaked hill. For their part the Prince's army lost 50 dead and 80 wounded. The twenty-minute battle had proved a stalemate, but it could have been turned to the Prince's advantage had not Murray decided to occupy Falkirk rather than follow-up the pursuit of the defeated army. The siege at Stirling was resumed without success and the Highland army eventually broke-off the operation and on 1 February retreated towards Perth

and Inverness, a day after Cumberland and most of the Royal army arrived at Linlithgow. Seven days later the Duke entered Perth and on the 21st the Jacobites occupied Inverness. From there they made a number of forays against the Great Glen posts, Fort Augustus falling after one week although Fort William proved harder to capture. Meanwhile Cumberland arrived in Aberdeen where he intended to spend the winter reorganizing his force and improving morale. The date was 27 February and Culloden was less than two months away.

▼ *'The Battle of Falkirk' (17 January 1746) by Lionel Edwards. The battle, a rearguard action to check Cumberland, lasted less than 30 minutes, and was remarkable for being one of the few occasions when infantry charged cavalry. When the Royal dragoons were within ten yards of the Jacobite line, a deadly volley cut down 80 troopers, forcing the remaining horsemen to flee into their own infantry hotly pursued by the Macdonalds. (Anne S. K. Brown Military Collection, Brown University)*

# THE OPPOSING COMMANDERS

## Charles Edward Stuart, the 'Young Pretender'

Charles Edward Stuart was just 25 years old when he led the Jacobite cause at Culloden, having been born on Old Year's Night, 1720, in the Italian city of Bologna. His mother, the Princess Maria Clementina Sobieska, daughter of Prince James Sobieski, was a descendant of the great John Sobieski, the saviour of Vienna from the Turks in September 1683. She had married the 31-year-old Prince James Francis Stuart, son of King James II, by proxy in May 1719, James still being in Spain in connection with the expedition to Scotland which had come to grief in the Pass of Glenshiel. Forlorn, he returned to his exile in Italy in September 1719 to find solace with his new bride. The birth of their son provided Jacobites everywhere with a cause for celebration – their hopes rested on the newborn as the one who would reclaim the throne of England.

From the beginning the child grew up in a world of intrigue and he was the intended victim of several kidnap plots. He was taught the skills of a soldier and at the ripe age of six could fire a gun and shoot a cross-bow with the accuracy expected of a much older boy; later he interested himself in the building of miniature fortifications. But apart from military matters and music, he showed flair for little else.

In 1734 the young teenager and his tutor, Murray, were invited by the Duke of Liria, son of the Duke of Berwick, to visit the Spanish forces under the King of Naples at the siege of Gaeta. Although it was intended that he be kept incognito and out of harm's way, he managed to visit the trenches at a time when the Spanish generals had retired during an artillery bombardment from the city, and officers and men alike praised his fearlessness. Yet in maturity the young Charles would show little evidence of military skill, unlike his father who had charged repeatedly with the *Maison du Roi* against Marlborough's lines at Malplaquet in 1708, and had witnessed the failed rebellion in 1715 and managed to escape in disguise.

The death of his mother in 1735 had a profound effect on the ambitious young man and the frustrations of his life in foreign exile made him yearn for action. Four years later his chance almost came when England declared war on Spain over the latter's interference in commerce and maritime issues. There was talk of an expedition to Scotland under the Earl Mareschal who had been appointed Commander-in-Chief in Scotland by James, but the Spanish were unwilling to lend their support. Charles then hoped to see action in France but this came to nothing and he had to bide his time in Rome, where he received word of the English victory under George II and his future opponent, Cumberland, at Dettingen in June 1743.

His patience was to be rewarded within two years. Military life and adventure had always held a keen appeal for Charles and he felt confident in his skill despite years of inaction in Italy where he had become increasingly despondent. Lacking intellect and wit, this handsome young man drew his inspiration from romance and adventure, and had an enormous charisma for his adoring followers.

Although he had been blooded at Gaeta, that experience paled to insignificance when compared to the events awaiting him at Prestonpans, Falkirk, and Culloden. As these battles would prove, Charles was not an opportunist. He preferred to hand the generalship to inferior subordinates such as John William O'Sullivan rather than to the more go-ahead Lord George Murray. These two contrasting figures cast a dominant shadow over Charles and against them he was unable to assert

◀ *Charles Edward Stuart, the 'Young Pretender'. witnessed war first-hand at the siege of Gaeta in 1734 and his successes at Prestonpans and Falkirk demonstrated strategic flair and gave him valuable experience and confidence. In fact, he almost succeeded in his objectives, but the responsibilities were too great for him and he failed to understand or acknowledge his subordinates. (Anne S. K. Brown Military Collection, Brown University)*

his authority. He demonstrated real strategic flair in conceiving and carrying out the rising in 1745, and 'thought of making war in terms of the chase: rapidity of movement, lightning thrusts, economy, sudden death.' But he lacked initiative for the grand tactic, the seeing of the whole event in the shape of things, unlike Montrose in the 1640s. For instance, after Falkirk he failed to order an advance against the demoralized English troops, or establish a defensive position at Falkirk to await Cumberland, choosing instead to renew siege operations against Stirling Castle, which were unsuccessful and led to eventual retreat to Perth and Inverness. The retreat was a blunder and it gave the English valuable time in which to reorganize their forces. At Culloden he failed to grasp the overall situation developing before him and his delay in ordering a charge cost him many lives.

In contrast to Cumberland, Charles showed

▶ 'William Augustus, Duke of Cumberland' (1721-65) by David Morier. The young prince was present at Dettingen and Fontenoy, where he was an inspiration to his men. He displayed energy and power in military affairs; in fact, with the exception of Lord Ligonier, he was probably the only man capable of inspiring the demoralized army and leading it to victory at Culloden. However, in spite of his generalship in Flanders in 1747 and later in the Seven Years War, his popularity never recovered after the Jacobite rebellion. (Anne S. K. Brown Military Collection, Brown University)

compassion, particularly at Prestonpans where he halted the Highland slaughter before it got out of hand and remained on the field providing assistance to the wounded of both armies. In Edinburgh, following the victory, he was opposed to a blockade against the castle, preferring instead to leave guards in place to 'keep in spies and keep out fresh butter and eggs'. He was well liked and had a dynamic magnetism that endeared him to his followers.

## William Augustus, Duke of Cumberland

On 15 April 1721 the citizens of London welcomed the news that the Prince of Wales and his wife, Caroline of Anspach, had become the proud parents of a new son, William Augustus, who would become the 'darling of the nation' in his youth, only to be despised in later life. From an early age he yearned to be a soldier perhaps even to become commander-in-chief of the British army, a position he attained in 1749. He must have heard many war stories from his father who had charged at Oudenarde, and from his grandfather who had fought in the ranks of William III's army at Neerwinden in 1693. Were it not for the excesses of the Royal army commanded by Cumberland following the victory at Culloden, the Duke might have gone down in history as one of England's finest eighteenth-century generals despite the failures at Fontenoy in 1745. His unpopularity following the Jacobite rebellion coupled with his ungainly figure provided carica-turists and satirists with a wealth of material. On the other hand, he was a soldier's general, loved by his men with whom he identified. His soldiers were his pride and joy and he was sympathetic to their needs. In return they showed confidence in his leadership, proclaiming 'Now, Billy, for Flan-ders!'

From an early age William Augustus displayed signs of leadership, as evidenced by the commands he would give to a miniature battalion of lads in the courtyard of St. James's, but he received no formal training in the elements of military science, although he mastered the art of hunting. He was created Duke of Cumberland in July 1726, but was always overshadowed by his brother Frederick, whom he despised. William's love of soldiering eventually got the upper hand and on his nine-teenth birthday in April 1740 he was appointed to the command of the Coldstream Guards, joining the regiment in camp at Hounslow. This was short-lived as he quit the camp and signed up as a volunteer aboard Sir John Norris's flagship, *Victory*, in which he served though without seeing any action. Subsequently he returned to his regiment, transferring to the First Guards in 1742. The following year found him in Germany with his father, the king, approaching the village of Dettin-gen with the allied army. James Wolfe, the future conqueror of Quebec, himself a young officer, said of the 22-two-year-old prince who fought the battle on the left of the first line of infantry: '[He] behaved as bravely as a man could do. He had a musket-ball through the calf of his leg. . . He gave his orders with a great deal of calmness, and seemed quite unconcerned.' Apparently William told the surgeon who was about to dress the wound

to tend to a nearby French officer whose wound was more serious. Unfortunately such benevolence was lost on the wounded clansmen who lay on the field at Culloden three years later. For his part in the victory at Dettingen, he was promoted to lieutenant-general and the following year saw him a captain-general of the British land forces at home. In that capacity he next tasted battle at Fontenoy where he was in sole command of the British contingent of the allied force against the French and he insisted on charging with his infantry. Wrote one who was there: 'He was the whole day in the thickest of the fire. When he saw the ranks breaking, he rode up and encouraged the soldiers in the most moving and expressive terms; called them countrymen.' Despite losing the battle Cumberland enabled his men to withdraw in order, for which he received much credit. Fon-tenoy and the British defeat was all the inspiration Charles Stuart needed for his endeavour in Scotland.

Fate brought the two Royal princes to Cullo-den, but Cumberland has been given the credit for making the battle possible; and for restoring confidence to the army, demoralized after its defeats at Prestonpans and Falkirk. The soldiers regained their self-respect and confidence thanks to the Duke's ability in morale boosting. This strict disciplinarian, who never shrank from using the lash, achieved something his predecessors had failed to achieve; he got his men to believe in themselves and in their ability to defeat the dreaded Highlanders. That the British Army was successful later in the Seven Years War owes something to Cumberland's reforms and training of the army and his love of its men. In the years following the battle, as commander-in-chief until his resignation in 1757, he continued to enjoy the respect of every soldier, from his generals to the lowliest man in the ranks, and even of his enemies such as Marshal Saxe. Indeed, Charles Stuart himself never shared his countrymen's hate for Cumberland, believing that a Royal prince could never have been truly responsible for the crimes committed after the battle, and he was afterwards opposed to any assassination plots against William Augustus. Yet the Duke's name lives on only as 'Butcher' Cumberland.

# THE OPPOSING ARMIES

The army of the British Government, and of its sovereign lord, King George II, which stood on the wet moor of Drummossie on the morning of 16 April 1746, can be considered a veteran force composed of experienced soldiers fresh from the campaigns on the Continent collectively known as the War of the Austrian Succession. Starting with Dettingen in 1743 and the events that culminated in the defeat at Fontenoy in May 1745, many of the regiments that fought with the Duke at Culloden were veterans of several actions. Any new recruits who had the misfortune to join up for the 'King's shilling' in the following months were soon bloodied in the débâcle at Prestonpans and the disaster at Falkirk.

## The Royal Army: Infantry

Throughout the eighteenth and much of the nineteenth century, the British army exhibited the extremes of British society, the officers drawn from the upper classes and the aristocracy, while the men in the ranks came from the lowest levels of society, often poor agricultural workers or urban unemployed in search of escape from poverty and starvation. The army drew most of its recruits from the ranks of the unemployed but regiments throughout the century were rarely at full strength and had to resort to 'beating up' for volunteers; a

▶A private of a battalion company in the King's army from the 1742 Clothing Book  The uniform is typical of the period: a tricorn felt hat trimmed with white lace, and a greatcoat of red cloth with chest lapels and huge cuffs but without a collar. The skirts were hooked back to show the regimental facings. The breeches and waistcoat were also red, the gaiters, worn high above the knee, were white. This soldier is from the 22nd Regiment. (Anne S. K. Brown Military Collection, Brown University)

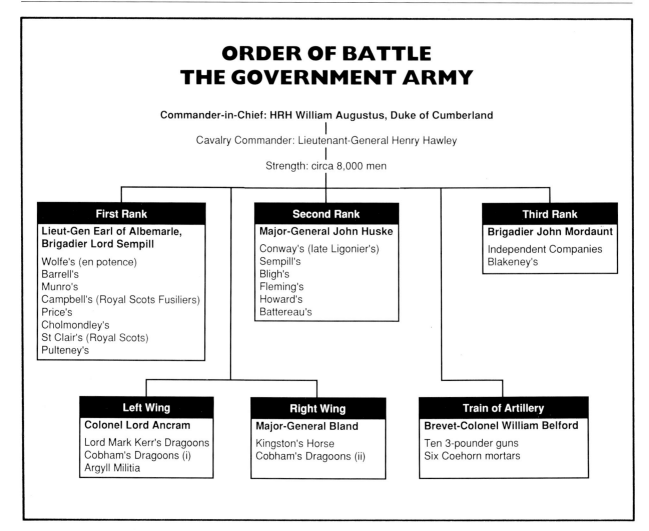

# ORDER OF BATTLE
# THE GOVERNMENT ARMY

**Commander-in-Chief: HRH William Augustus, Duke of Cumberland**

Cavalry Commander: Lieutenant-General Henry Hawley

Strength: circa 8,000 men

**First Rank**

**Lieut-Gen Earl of Albemarle, Brigadier Lord Sempill**

Wolfe's (en potence)
Barrell's
Munro's
Campbell's (Royal Scots Fusiliers)
Price's
Cholmondley's
St Clair's (Royal Scots)
Pulteney's

**Second Rank**

**Major-General John Huske**

Conway's (late Ligonier's)
Sempill's
Bligh's
Fleming's
Howard's
Battereau's

**Third Rank**

**Brigadier John Mordaunt**

Independent Companies
Blakeney's

**Left Wing**

**Colonel Lord Ancram**

Lord Mark Kerr's Dragoons
Cobham's Dragoons (i)
Argyll Militia

**Right Wing**

**Major-General Bland**

Kingston's Horse
Cobham's Dragoons (ii)

**Train of Artillery**

**Brevet-Colonel William Belford**

Ten 3-pounder guns
Six Coehorn mortars

---

subaltern, an NCO or two and a drummer were sent to recruit, their successes coming particularly during winter and after harvest time when large numbers of men had been laid-off. When the man 'signed up' he had to swear an oath that he was a Protestant, had 'no rupture' was not 'troubled with fits', and had to have perfect use of his limbs. He had also to be 5 feet 6 inches in height. Once in the army, the new recruit was allocated to a regiment, and this became his home for life unless he was invalided out, deserted or was killed. Other troops were 'drafted'; that is, men from old, established regiments were drawn together to form new battalions, as happened in Flanders in 1743.

In 1745, however, with the Jacobite emergency in the north, other inducements to join the army were quickly introduced to fill the ranks of the depleted home-based regiments. On 6 September,

every recruit who joined the Guards before the 24th of the month was offered a bounty of £6, and those joining in the last six days of September were offered £4. Elsewhere various noblemen offered to raise and equip two regiments of horse and thirteen regiments of foot, and a group of volunteer horseman was organized in Yorkshire.

According to the *Army List* of 1745, there were 56 regiments of Foot, three regiments of Foot Guards and two regiments of Grenadier Guards, 14 regiments of Dragoons, and eight regiments of Cavalry. However, new regiments were raised during 1745 and 1746, increasing the number of infantry regiments to 80. The same publication lists the total number of troops in Great Britain in 1745 as 18,507.

Regiments were identified by the name of their colonels; thus, the 1st of Foot was St. Clair's; the

*Uniforms of the Government forces: 1, Drummer, Barrell's Regiment; 2, Officer, Royal North British Fusiliers; 3, Corporal, Munro's Regiment. (G. A. Embleton)*

▲ *A private in a grenadier company from the 1742 Clothing Book, representing the uniform worn by such companies at Culloden, with a broad leather shoulder belt supporting a large black pouch, a broad waist-belt carrying a small sword and the bayonet in a frog on the left side. The 23rd Regiment served on garrison duty in England during the rising in anticipation of a possible French invasion, although their colonel, Brigadier Huske, fought at Falkirk and commanded the second line at Culloden. (Anne S. K. Brown Military Collection, Brown University)*

13th, Pulteney's, and so on. Each regiment consisted of ten companies of 70 men. With officers, the regiment was set at 815 men, but rarely did the units maintain those numbers and many of the regiments at Culloden were little stronger than about 400 men. In a dragoon regiment, there were six troops of 59 men, making a total of 435 men and officers. The forces serving in Flanders in 1745 had twelve companies of 70 men each per regiment, while the cavalry had six troops with more men, 75, in each. The total number of troops serving in Flanders at that time was estimated at 28,026 officers and men. Other British contingents were serving in Ireland, Minorca, Gibraltar, the American colonies, and the Caribbean. At Culloden it is estimated that Cumberland commanded 6,400 infantry and 2,400 cavalry.

Once the new recruit arrived at the barracks or garrison, he was presented with a 'good, Full Bodied Coth Coat well Lin'd' of red serge faced with the colour of his regiment, a waistcoat, kersey breeches, strong stockings and shoes, shirts, neckcloth and a 'Strong Hat well Lac'd. Caps to Fusiliers,' but these would have to last. From then on his living conditions were miserable, and if he did not toe the line he would be disciplined with the cat-o'-nine tails. His food was abysmal and he was expected to pay for it. Other deductions from his meagre pay went towards the regimental surgeon, the regimental agent, and towards the upkeep of Chelsea Hospital. The Scottish emergency brought some relief to the common soldiers in terms of a new flannel waistcoat presented to each man by the Quakers, and in London a subscription was started in order to provide a blanket and two paillasses for each tent, a pair of worsted gloves to each man, and thirty watchcoats for each battalion.

Fortunately for the soldiers who fought at Culloden, few had lingered for long periods in filthy barracks and their discipline had been honed by their endeavours on the Continent. Armed with a firelock, the British battalions in the Allied line at Dettingen gave a 'regular, swift and continuous fire' in volleys that devastated the French. At Fontenoy, the British troops had been badly hit by French artillery and cavalry, a fact no doubt noted by Cumberland. However, the failure at Fontenoy had a psychological effect on the soldiers that may have contributed to the setbacks in Scotland. When Cumberland again resumed control of the army at Aberdeen early in 1746, he set about instilling confidence in the troops and initiated a series of new tactics for the infantry. In the three months between Falkirk and Culloden, the soldiers were put through intensive drilling, particularly a new method of bayonet drill, to restore confidence.

Aside from the new bayonet tactic (to lunge at the opponent to one's immediate right) the army at Culloden followed the tactics laid down in the 1728 Regulations, and to a lesser extent the numerous minor manual and platoon exercises and engraved plates of such. For instance, in 1745 a series of plates appeared showing the several 'positions of a Soldier under arms'. The chief weapon of the British army at this time as depicted in these exercises was the sealed pattern Long Land musket introduced around 1745, also known as the 'Brown Bess'. It had a 46-inch barrel with a long fore end and a wooden ramrod. With a bore of .75in, its bullets were 13 or 14 to the pound. It used flint and steel to generate a spark igniting the charge of gunpowder in the pan; this was connected by a small channel to the musket barrel wherein lay the main charge. The cartridge was made up of a tube of strong cartridge paper sealed with thread at both ends. It enclosed six to eight drams of powder and a lead bullet. After biting off the rear end of the cartridge, the soldier squeezed a small amount of powder into the pan and emptied the rest into the barrel. The bullet was next inserted and rammed down with the paper cartridge serving as wadding (although banging the butt of the musket on the ground served the same purpose and also sent powder into the pan, thus eliminating the necessity of placing the powder by hand into the pan). A trained soldier could fire four to five rounds a minute, but the musket was generally inaccurate over fifty yards owing to the looseness of the bullet in the bore, and there were also frequent misfires as a result of the failure of the powder to penetrate into the pan. The soldiers in the Royal army were issued twenty-four rounds. Along with a socket bayonet with a triangular-section blade of seventeen inches in length, the

▲ *Musket exercises, 1745. The Government soldiers at the time of the Rising would have been familiar with these exercises for the use of the firelock musket, and the concentrated fire employed at Culloden by the front-line regiments followed strict principles laid down for firing. Much of the time spent at Aberdeen in the winter of 1746 would have been given over to the drill of such movements and the new bayonet tactics. (Anne S. K. Brown Military Collection, Brown University)*

infantryman carried a hanger with a polished brass hilt and a blade some 27 inches long. This was carried in a black leather scabbard fastened to a 2-inch wide belt.

## The Royal Army: Cavalry

The cavalry had arrived in Scotland in the middle of January 1746, having spent the last few years on garrison duty or policing the southern English

coast for smugglers. Some had been bloodied earlier on a snowy December night above the moors of Westmorland at Clifton, near Penrith, when four dismounted troops of English cavalry attacked a small force of retreating Highlanders. The affair was over in a few minutes with no clear winner. As a consequence, the cavalry at Culloden were hardly combat-experienced.

Made up of volunteers, who were not to exceed 5 feet 8 inches in height, most had barely progressed beyond basic training. This consisted of the care of the horse, cleaning stables and undergoing the same basic training of a foot soldier. The horses were not to be older than four years nor over 15 hands high. Occasionally small and lighter horses were bought 'keeping however, still to the black Cullour'. Once the trooper had been taught to control his horse, he was taught to ride and then to perform mounted evolutions such as opening and closing rank and wheeling in line.

*◄Uniforms of the Government forces: 1, Grenadier, Ligonier's Regiment; 2, Gunner, Royal Artillery; 3, Officers, Cobham's Dragoons. (G. A. Embleton)*

*►A trooper of the 13th Dragoons as depicted in the 1742* Clothing Book, *in uniform and equipment worn at Culloden. The Regiment fought at Prestonpans where its colonel, James Gardiner, was killed, and at Falkirk, but was at Edinburgh during the Culloden campaign to guard against the passage of English Jacobites. After the battle the Regiment was involved in searching for fugitives and guarding prisoners. (Anne S. K. Brown Military Collection, Brown University)*

The next stage for a dragoon recruit was to learn to fire his carbine and pistols from the saddle.

Emphasis was laid upon swordsmanship, and new tactics were periodically introduced. On 10 March 1746, the following order was given to the dragoons in Scotland: 'H.R.H. orders that all Officers of Dragoons who may happen to be at the head of a squadron, party or detachment of Dragoons, when there may be likelihood of engaging the enemy, are to make their men sling their firelocks just before they draw their sword, and to take particular care to hinder their men from handling their pistols, unless when in pursuit of a broken enemy, running from them.'

The standard cavalry firearms were the Land Service pistol and the carbine. The pistol had a 12-inch barrel of 17 or carbine bore and a heavy butt. With the standard flint carbine lock, the overall length was between 18 and 20 inches. The other dragoon firearm was the carbine, with a barrel length of between 27 and 36 inches, a 17 bore and twenty bullets to the pound. The Duke of Kingston's Light Horse, which was raised for the Jacobite Rebellion and then disbanded later in 1746, had a shorter carbine. The trooper's other weapon was his sword which had a heavy brass bowl guard, a brass ball pommel and a straight 35-inch long blade, which was carried in a black leather scabbard.

## The Royal Army: Artillery

At Culloden, it was the artillery which was to prove the most devastating weapon against the ranks of the Jacobite infantry. The ten 3-pounder guns under William Belford drawn up in pairs at intervals between the six front regiments, and the six Coehorn mortars, in two batteries of three, were extremely effective against lines of stationary troops: 'The guns were so exceedingly well plied that they made dreadful lanes through some of the clan regiments', wrote one observer.

However, the success of the artillery in the battle can be attributed to the lessons learnt earlier in the rebellion. Prior to the battle the state of the artillery had been described as deplorable. It had performed poorly at Prestonpans, but allowance must be made for the absence of trained gunners – the guns were in fact served by seamen. Some success was achieved by six 18-pounders upon the crumbling walls of Carlisle in late December 1745, which forced the city to surrender. At Falkirk the artillery, a strange assortment of ten cannon, fared little better under Captain Archibald Cuningham; the civilian drivers of most of the guns fled the field, and many of the guns became stuck in a bog. Of the pieces that had been with Hawley's army, seven were captured. One obvious need was greater mobility for the artillery, and this was addressed in the weeks following Falkirk.

In 1743 the Royal Regiment of Artillery consisted of eight companies, only one of which was present at Culloden, the others being at Woolwich, on the Continent or in North America. A company consisted of approximately seven officers (captain and lieutenants), three sergeants and three corporals, eight bombardiers, 20 gunners, 62 matrosses, and 2 drummers, a total of 105 officers and men. The principal weapon at this time was the 3-pounder smooth-bore muzzle-loader on its distinctive and clumsy double-bracket carriage. The range of fire was about 500 yards and it fired two kinds of missile: round iron shot and canister, which was filled with metal frag-

ments. The Coehorn mortars had a calibre of $4\frac{2}{5}$ inches. Various smallarms were also carried by the men including halberds, brass-hilted swords and muskets.

## The Allied Contingent

The Royal Army during the period of the rebellion contained elements of foreign troops. Under the terms of a previous treaty 6,000 Dutch soldiers had been ordered to England at the

▼'British 1st Grenadier', an original water-colour based on Bernard Lens's drawing for The Grenadiers' Exercise of the Grenado, in his Majesty's first Regiment of Foot-Guards, *which was dedicated to the Duke of Cumberland in 1735.* *The large pouch in front held grenades, but there is no evidence to suggest that grenades were ever employed during the Scottish campaign. (Anne S. K. Brown Military Collection, Brown University)*

beginning of the campaign and a Dutch regiment had been on board a ship in the Firth of Forth during the battle of Prestonpans but had been warned against landing. Most of the Dutch forces were garrisoned at Newcastle under Field Marshal Wade, but were rendered immobile when the Irish troops from Louis XV's army landed, having agreed not to raise arms against the French king following the Dutch surrender of Tournai a few months earlier. For the duration of the Scottish troubles five thousand Hessians under Prince Frederick were taken into British pay.

▼ *Samuel McPherson of the Highland Regiment, who was shot for desertion in 1743. His dress is typical of that worn by the independent companies and militia at Culloden. He is wearing a corporal's shoulder-knot and is carrying a broadsword, musket and bayonet, a pistol suspended from a narrow belt, and a dirk next to the sporran. (Anne S. K. Brown Military Collection, Brown University)*

Having landed at Leith they originally deployed at Perth but later fell back on Stirling where they refused to relieve Blair Castle.

However, the main non-English troops serving with Cumberland's army were the Independent Companies, a number of volunteers and auxiliaries raised by various loyalist clan leaders, and the Argyll or Campbell Militia. At the outset of the rebellion, the Government delegated Duncan Forbes of Culloden and Archibald, 3rd Duke of Argyll to raise twenty Independent Companies of Highlanders and a Regiment of Militia loyal to the Hanoverian Succession. Initially the task of the Companies was to disrupt Jacobite recruitment and taxation, to 'live at discretion in the counties which the rebels have left'. Each company was made up of a captain, lieutenant, ensign, four sergeants, four corporals, one drummer, one piper, and one hundred private men who were to be 'regularly enlisted, subsisted, paid, armed, equipped and clothed'. The main weapon was the broadsword in addition to side-pistols, targets and dirks. The target or shield was 19 to 21 inches in diameter made of wood covered with leather and having brass studs. All the companies appear to have worn Highland dress and their only emblem of allegiance was the black cockade and red cross in the bonnet. At Culloden the Independent Companies with the exception of one detachment were held in reserve and saw little action.

Not so the Argyll Militia, a regiment in itself and quite distinct from the Independent Companies. Raised by the Duke of Argyll, it played a particularly prominent part in breaking down the walls on the left flank and providing flanking fire for Cumberland's dragoons to outflank the Jacobites. They were ably assisted in this task by the small detachment from the Independent Companies. The regiment numbered some 1,000 members of the Clan Campbell in ten companies by the end of 1745. Their recruitment, terms of service, discipline, pay and subsistence was similar to the Independent Companies. Originally the intention was to cloth all Scottish loyalists in a short red coat and long waistcoat, belted plaid, red and white hose and a round blue bonnet, but due to delays and shortages the uniform was never issued. As a consequence, each militiaman wore his Highland dress and tartan with the Hanoverian black cockade and large coloured cross on the bonnet. Arms were issued, the main weapons being a musket, bayonet, broadsword and side-pistol which served to complement their own target and dirk. At Culloden, the regiment's strength was 630 officers and other ranks but the unit was disbanded in August 1746 although some men joined the new independent companies and other new corps such as Loudon's Highlanders and the Black Watch.

## The Jacobite Army

The army that gathered around Prince Charles Edward Stuart in 1745 to achieve the restoration of King James VIII did not exist prior to 19 August 1745 when, at Glenfinnan, Charles, acting as Regent, raised the Stuart Royal Standard. Over the next few weeks the main elements of what was to become the Jacobite army came together, and at its peak at Falkirk reached a maximum strength of 8,000 men. Even this however was a small fraction of the fighting potential of the Highlands, estimated at more than 32,000 men. On the orders of the clan leaders, hundreds of clansmen from the Camerons, Macphersons, Appin Stewarts, Keppoch, Glengarry and the Macdonalds of Clanranald, came forth. They were joined by feudal levies such as the Atholl brigade, made up of men who served their lords under the terms of their land tenure. Others were volunteers, one example being the Manchester Regiment. While numbers varied from regiment to regiment, for the most part they were each approximately 500 men strong. Two of the largest clan regiments were Lochiel's Camerons and the Macdonalds of Glengarry. Clans such as the Campbells, Grants, Munros and

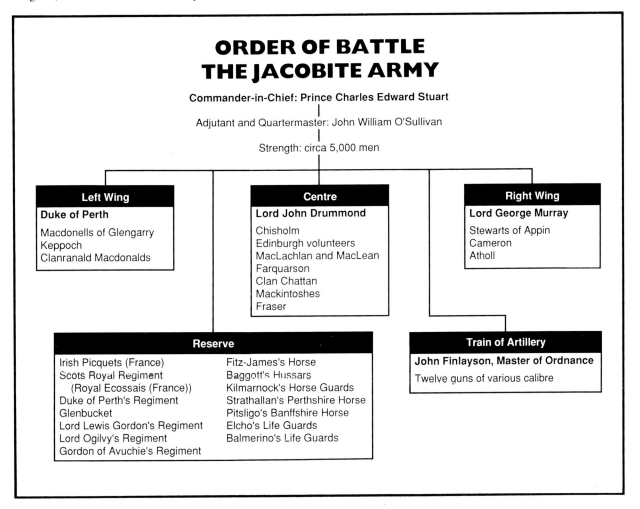

# ORDER OF BATTLE
# THE JACOBITE ARMY

**Commander-in-Chief: Prince Charles Edward Stuart**

Adjutant and Quartermaster: John William O'Sullivan

Strength: circa 5,000 men

**Left Wing**

**Duke of Perth**

Macdonells of Glengarry
Keppoch
Clanranald Macdonalds

**Centre**

**Lord John Drummond**

Chisholm
Edinburgh volunteers
MacLachlan and MacLean
Farquarson
Clan Chattan
Mackintoshes
Fraser

**Right Wing**

**Lord George Murray**

Stewarts of Appin
Cameron
Atholl

**Reserve**

Irish Picquets (France)
Scots Royal Regiment
   (Royal Ecossais (France))
Duke of Perth's Regiment
Glenbucket
Lord Lewis Gordon's Regiment
Lord Ogilvy's Regiment
Gordon of Avuchie's Regiment

Fitz-James's Horse
Baggott's Hussars
Kilmarnock's Horse Guards
Strathallan's Perthshire Horse
Pitsligo's Banffshire Horse
Elcho's Life Guards
Balmerino's Life Guards

**Train of Artillery**

**John Finlayson, Master of Ordnance**

Twelve guns of various calibre

Sutherlands were Whigs in political sympathy and did not join the Prince, while others joined the Hanoverian government or abstained from intervention. Some regiments like Ogilvy's had two battalions with about 300 men in each although at Culloden the combined battalions totalled only some 500. The muster-roll of this regiment mentions 73 officers, 20 sergeants, 5 drummers and 528 privates. Of the officers, one was the colonel (Lord Ogilvy), two were lieutenant-colonels, a colonel serving as aide-de-camp, two majors, an adjutant, a paymaster, 21 captains and the same number of lieutenants, nineteen ensigns, two chaplains and two surgeons. These officers, all kilted (like the privates) in the Ogilvy tartan, were farmers or merchants, the men being labourers, craftsmen, domestic servants and land-holders. One fundamental problem for the Jacobite army was the lack of officers, and Charles's choice of Irish and French officers, which caused much disagreement among Scots.

The lack of professionalism and training of the

◀ *The Young Pretender depicted in a contemporary engraving. At Culloden he was armed with a pair of silver-mounted pistols and a leather target bearing a silver head of Medusa. In this scene he holds a Highland broadsword and at his feet are a pair of crossed pistols and a plain target. (Anne S. K. Brown Military Collection, Brown University)*

Jacobite infantry was frequently apparent. The Keppoch and Glengarry Macdonalds lacked proper discipline and were considered uncontrollable by their colonels. In one incident, Keppoch's men, having shot the Marquis of Lothian's fallow deer, turned their guns on their officers who had shouted to them to stop, but no casualties were reported. In 1745 a Government agent in Durham reported that the clansmen were totally out of hand and that their officers, fearing a revolt, indulged them.

Unlike the government army, discipline among the Jacobites was not imposed by the lash; morale was maintained and personal loyalty instilled by their leaders. Although desertion was rare during the invasion into England, the 1746 campaign in Scotland saw some clansmen leaving the army for more pressing matters. Deserters arrested were not executed but rather persuaded to rejoin. As for looting and rapine, there were no reports of such activities during the invasion into England owing to the regular method of financing the army by

▶*A gentleman of the Clan Ogilvy in a Victorian illustration by R. R. McIan, based on a contemporary portrait of James, Earl of Perth, Lieutenent-General. He is wearing trews which were the usual dress of gentlemen. The Ogilvy Regiment, which was not a Highland corps, was raised in Angus and joined the Prince's army at Edinburgh in October 1745. (Anne S. K. Brown Military Collection, Brown University)*

◄*Clothing of the Jacobite forces: 1, Colonel, Lord Ogilvy's Regiment; 2, Junior Officer, Clan (Fraser) regiment; 3, front rank man, Clan regiment. (G. A. Embleton)*

►*A member of the Highland Regiment of 1743 who was shot for desertion. In 1739 several independent companies of highlanders were formed into the Highland Regiment, or Black Watch. While red tunics were issued, the figure in this contemporary engraving wears typical Highland garb with only the initials 'GR' on the ammunition pouch giving a clue to his allegiance. (Anne S. K. Brown Military Collection)*

collecting public funds, such as sequestered estates and taxes.

Unlike their opponents, the Jacobite army had an array of weapons at its disposal. The clansmen wielded basket-hilted broadswords, dirks, muskets and pistols. Of the traditional clan weapons, the Lochaber axe was rarely used during the campaign, but the target or shield was carried by both Highlanders and Lowlanders. A few bayonets were also in evidence. Firearms came from France and Spain but were in short supply as was ammunition, which meant that the soldiers entering England in 1745 were issued 'twelve shot' – twelve lead balls, powder and paper for securing the charge – with restrictions on wastage. This was considered meagre by contemporary standards, leading some to suggest that the Jacobite army could not fight a pitched battle.

One surviving account describes the method of a Highland attack at the time: '[The Highlander] when descending to battle, was to place his bonnet on his head with an emphatic "scrug"; his second, to cast off or throw back his plaid; his third to incline his body horizontally forward, cover it with his target, rush to within 50 paces of the enemy's line, discharge and drop his fusee or musket; his fourth to dart within 12 paces, discharge and fling his claw-butted steel stocked pistols at the foeman's head; his fifth to draw claymore and dirk at him!' Another account states that the Highlanders 'stooped below the charged bayonets, they tossed them upward by the target, dirking the front rank man with the left hand, while stabbing or hewing down the rear rank man with the right; thus, as usual in all Highland onsets, the whole body of soldiers was broken, trod underfoot, and dispersed in a moment'. (All this while charging barefoot and refusing to wear shoes even on the march.)

As for the Prince's artillery, which performed poorly at Culloden, he had to hand thirteen pieces of cannon of varying calibre, the largest being a 4-pounder. The different calibres must have created ammunition supply problems. Six were Swedish guns ranging in size from 2- to 4-pounders. The remaining weapons, six 1-pounder Coehorns, came from the Tower of London, having been captured at Prestonpans. This odd assortment of cannon were manned by inexperienced gunners, and at Culloden some of the weapons on the left-wing were manned by volunteers who succeeded in firing only two rounds; the guns in the centre did succeed in killing five or six redcoats.

In terms of cavalry, the Prince could count on five troops of horse, but each varied in strength from month to month. Elcho's Life Guards, around 160 in all, consisted of seventy men and their servants under five officers in October 1745, but at Culloden less than half were present. In their special uniform of blue trimmed with red, they were regarded as a key corps. In contrast, Lord Balmerino's Horse numbered only 40 troopers who, like Elcho's, fought dismounted at Culloden; 16 troopers were also with the Prince in reserve. The horse grenadiers were commanded by the 37-year old Earl of Kilmarnock, but they also included the Perthshire Horse, 130 men organized into two troops under Lord Strathallan. At Culloden, the Perthshire Horse were stationed to the left of Lord Pitsligo's Horse, made up chiefly of gentlemen from Aberdeenshire and Banffshire and totalling about 160 under the command of the 60-year old lord. The final Scottish cavalry contingent were hussars under the command of an Irish officer, Colonel Baggot. (John Murray of Brougton, the Prince's secretary, had been the original commander of this force, but missed the battle due to illness.) The hussars were considered poorly trained and were regarded as the weakest arm of the cavalry. Like the Life Guards, Pitsligo's men were considered the finest of the Jacobite cavalry, although at Culloden most of the Jacobite cavalry were forced to fight on foot and could not demonstrate their riding prowess.

As for pay, according to Lord Elcho a captain was paid 2s 6d per day, a lieutenant 2s, an ensign 1s 6d and a private 6d, although Lord Balmerino states that the 'gentlemen' received 2s per day. At the trials following the end of the rebellion, it was mentioned that privates in the Jacobite army received a daily allowance of 7d or 8d. For the cavalry slightly more was paid, sergeants receiving 1s 8d and rankers 1s. While on paper these were the expected amounts, as the campaign wore on and money became scarce, payments fell into arrears, the men receiving meals in lieu.

### The Irish and French Contingents

At Culloden the Prince was served on the left flank by a Franco-Irish cavalry regiment, Fitz-James's Horse, which had landed in Scotland in late 1745 from Ostend. Under its commander, Colonel Robert O'Shea, it numbered only 70 at the battle, many of the troopers having surrendered on the march northwards out of England. They were further handicapped by their horses having been captured at sea. Nevertheless, they were the only cavalry regiment on the Jacobite side at Culloden to fight the whole battle on horseback. The regiment was clothed in red coats turned up with blue, yellow skin breeches, black tricorn hats laced with silver, and beneath their coats black-painted iron breastplates. Their weapons were carbines or muskets, pistols and straight brass-hilted swords.

▶ *'Clan Forbes' by R. R. McIan. It is generally agreed that no clan tartans were worn in the battle, and that after the failed attack on the Royal camp the night before Culloden, and the subsequent turmoil, many clansmen would have presented an uncharacteristically shoddy appearance due to the haste in which they formed up. The only distinguishing mark of the Jacobites was the white cockade worn in the bonnet; on one occasion a wounded Highlander, having lost his hat, was asked which side he fought on. (Anne S. K. Brown Military Collection, Brown University)*

◀ 'A young man of the Clan Cameron', by R. R. McIan. He is wearing the traditional dress of belted plaid (in Gaelic plaide means blanket). This consisted of a rectangle of cloth six yards long and six feet wide. A lower pleated part made up the skirt which was held up by a belt. The gun, of Spanish manufacture, is typical of the weapons used by the Highlanders in both the '15 and '45 Rebellions. (Anne S. K. Brown Military Collection, Brown University)

Of the original four squadrons, only one had landed at Aberdeen, numbering about 120-130 men, the other three along with picquets of five Irish regiments of foot still being aboard transports. Unfortunately for the Prince, two of these transports were captured by Commodore Knowles on February 24. This was a bitter loss, for the regiment had considerable experience in battle, having seen recent service in Italy and on the Rhine with the French army.

While the majority of the Irish picquets and Fitz-James's Horse were captured, about 359 men and 36 officers in all, a number of men from various regiments of the Irish brigade did see action in the campaign. About 750 soldiers from the Irish regiments commanded by Brigadier

▶Private soldier of Roth's Irish Regiment, circa 1740. The Irish picquets who fought at Culloden for the Jacobite cause were formed from three Irish regiments in French service – Dillon's, Ruth's and Lally's. The men wore red coats with the facings of their different regiments. (Anne S. K. Brown Military Collection)

Stapleton and Lord John Drummond's French Royal Scots had landed on the east coast at the end of 1745. The picquets were mainly Irishmen drawn from the six Irish infantry regiments in French service, and they along with their officers had distinguished themselves earlier in the year at Fontenoy against the same enemy. According to one eyewitness of the Irish troops who were captured at sea, 'the men are all clothed in red, and their officers have mostly gold-laced hats. To speak impartially the officers are as proper men as ever I saw in my life, being mostly 5 feet 10 or 6 feet high and between 40 and 50 years of age; and the common soldiers are very good-like men, and if they had landed might have done a great deal of mischief.'

# CULLODEN: THE APPROACH MARCH

On 30 January 1746, with the unfortunate Hawley, the loser at Falkirk, as his commander of cavalry, the Duke of Cumberland, Commander-in-Chief of the Royal army, arrived by ship at Leith, the port of Edinburgh. His predecessors, Cope and Hawley, having failed to remove the Jacobite threat, the Westminster government considered the Duke to be the only man left for the job, and the Duke himself was determined to bring the Jacobites to battle and defeat them once and for all. With the onset of winter, he decided to move his troops north to Aberdeen and await better weather before proceeding. During this respite, the army was increased with the addition of 5,000 Hessian mercenaries under Prince Frederick of Hesse, who took up a position to the south to block any retreat by the Pretender's forces. More importantly, the Duke used the time to drill his troops in new infantry tactics. The bitter experiences at Prestonpans and Falkirk had shown that the bayonet was no match for a frontal attack by a Highlander armed with a target which could parry the bayonet. However, some shrewd thinker observed that the attacking Highlander was unprotected on his left side; therefore, if each soldier engaged the enemy immediately to his right rather than directly to his front, he would be covering his neighbour, and the Highlander, carrying his target in his right hand, could be caught. The extreme left-hand file presumably was covered by an officer or sergeant standing on the flank.

By 8 April the weather had improved to the extent that the roads were clear of snow and the River Spey was fordable. Supplies had been gathered and the army moved off, reaching Cullen by the 11th, where the Duke's force was joined by Albemarle with six battalions and two cavalry regiments that had been wintering at Strathbogie, and General Mordaunt's reserve force of three battalions and four guns from Old Meldrum. Three days later the army crossed the Spey,

undeterred by Lord John Drummond's 2,000 Highlanders who had been holding the riverside, but quickly withdrew leaving the path open to Nairn. On the 15th, the bivouacked army celebrated the Duke's 25th birthday with a helping of liquor for all ranks, two gallons of brandy having been issued to each regiment. By now Drummond's troops and those of the Duke of Perth had reached Culloden in a dejected state. Morale in the Royal army was high, however, and the soldiers appreciated the fact that Cumberland had marched part of the way with them on foot.

During the period that the English troops had been moving north the Jacobites, farther to the west, had been subduing the Highland posts at Ruthven, Fort William and Fort Augustus and had now returned up the Great Glen to Inverness. It had become clear to Charles that he would have to weather a general action to achieve his goal, and the call went out to rally his supporters, many of whom had returned to their homes. On 14 April, to the sound of the pipes, the Jacobite army marched eastward out of the town for five miles towards Drummossie Moor where they camped in the woods and fields adjacent to the moor close to Culloden House. At a council of war it was decided to attempt a surprise night attack on the Royal camp, but the plan was made too hastily to succeed. Late on the following day the force moved towards Nairn, but the columns failed to keep their distance and the subsequent delay and confusion wrought havoc among troops unaccustomed to such a delicate operation. The Jacobites were discovered and forced to retreat to Culloden which they reached in the early hours of the 16th, tired and forlorn. To their consternation they found that the supplies had been left behind at Inverness, and as there was no time to retrieve them, some of the men lay down on the cold ground to sleep, while others went out to forage. Prince Charles did not return to Culloden until

▶'*Cumberland on Horseback*', *painted by Morier in 1751. At the time of the battle Cumberland weighed all of eighteen stones, but the artist has drawn a large horse so as not to emphasize its overweight master. After the battle every commanding officer received an oval medal to be worn around the neck on a crimson ribbon. The medal bore a profile of the Duke with the name 'Cumberland' inscribed above his head. The reverse bore an image of Apollo standing upon a dying dragon. (Anne S. K. Brown Military Collection, Brown University)*

7.00 a.m., having ridden twelve miles to Inverness and back in search of food for his troops. He even threatened to burn down the town should they refuse his request, but before he had time to carry out this threat the Duke of Perth, fearing an imminent attack, persuaded him to return to Drummossie.

There, Murray asked the Prince whether he still planned to fight a battle that day. Charles replied that there was really no alternative given the fatigued condition of his officers and men who would be in no state to conduct an orderly retreat from the Royal army. Murray suggested three

possibilities: to retire to Inverness and prepare for a siege; or the army could disperse into the Highlands and await another chance in the following spring; finally, if Charles wanted a battle the army should cross the Nairn to the more suitable position that had been reconnoitred the day before and deemed unfit for cavalry. These alternatives were dismissed despite Murray's suggestion that a battle on Drummossie Moor could end in defeat and the loss of Inverness. Another member of the Prince's staff, the Marquis d'Eguilles, special envoy of Louis XV, also commented on the poor condition of the troops and urged the alternative

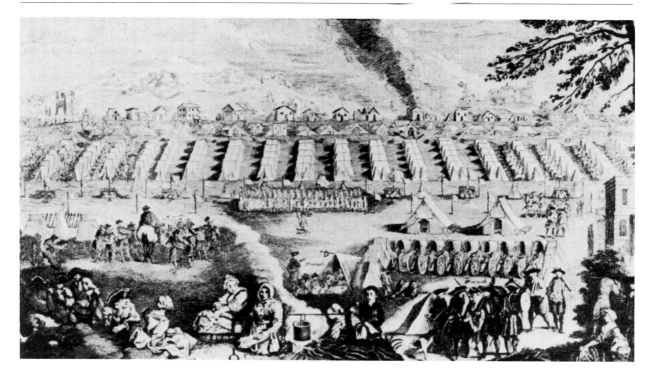

◄A French and Scottish Camp as depicted in a contemporary engraving. It is doubtful whether any of the Jacobite camps presented such an orderly appearance, and the engraver has over-emphasized the presence of the French troops purely for propaganda purposes. According to the Chevalier de Johnstone the Jacobites occupied the field at Culloden on 13 April without tents or any shelter and spent three nights on the bare ground in the open. (Anne S. K. Brown Military Collection, Brown University)

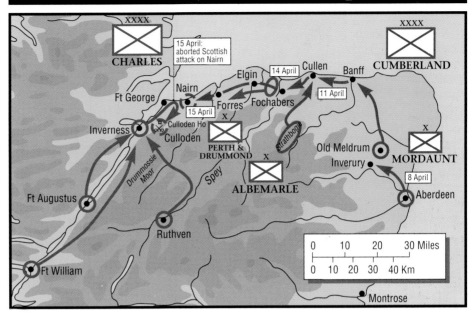

# The March to Culloden, 8-15 April 1746

◄The Crossing of the Spey. On 14 April 1746 the Royal army under Cumberland, having spent the winter at Aberdeen, continued its march towards Culloden to the accompaniment of 225 kettledrums! On the 14th they crossed the River Spey and came into contact with Jacobite outposts. The river was forded in three places without the expected opposition, although a dragoon and three women were drowned. (Anne S. K. Brown Military Collection, Brown University)

▼Culloden House, the home of Duncan Forbes, the Lord President of the Court of Session and a supporter of the Hanoverian cause. Forbes tried in vain to dissuade many clans from joining

Prince Charles. Attacked in 1715, another attempt to capture the house failed in October 1745. Charles slept there on Monday, 14 April 1746 and was there again briefly on the morning of Culloden.

After the battle Forbes's steward hid eighteeen fugitives there for three days until they were discovered and executed. (Anne S. K. Brown Military Collection, Brown University)

field, but to no avail, despite a plea on bended knee.

Early on that cold rainy morning of Wednesday the 16th, the Royalist troops struck camp, having eaten sparingly and drunk some brandy. Fresh from a good night's sleep, they were moving off towards the moorland around Drummossie and Culloden by 5 a.m. On the moor, which was well suited to the manoeuvres of foot and cavalry, the government army had the pick of the land and deployed on firm, level ground. The battle was now inevitable.

The Battle of Culloden on the 16. of April 1746.

# THE BATTLE OF CULLODEN

When the Royal army was within four miles of Drummossie its advance guard was sighted by Jacobite pickets. The Duke's informers reported that the rebel army was moving into position about a mile from Culloden House. At about eleven o'clock under heavy showers the two armies came into sight of each other across two miles of the open moorland. Cumberland ordered his columns to halt and take up their battle formations. As organized by his staff, Lieutenant-Generals Hawley and Albemarle, Major-General Bland and Brigadier Lord Sempill, three lines of troops deployed along a 700-yard front between the walls of cultivated enclosures and moved to within 500 yards of the rebel lines. In the front line running from right to left were: Pulteney's St. Clair's Royals, Cholmondeley's, Price's, Campbell's Royal Scots Fusiliers, Munro's and Barrell's. A hundred or so yards behind, forming the second line, from right to left were the regiments of Howard, Fleming, Bligh, Sempill, Ligonier and Wolfe, all commanded by Major-General Huske. Bringing up the rear were Blakeney's and Battereau's Regiments under the command of Brigadier Mordant. On the flanks, the cavalry were arrayed with Viscount Cobham's and Lord Mark Kerr's dragoons, directed by Colonel Lord Ancram, on the left with elements of the Argyll Militia. They took up position just within the Leanach enclosure and out of sight of the main Jacobite force. Kingston's Horse took up their position on the right flank under Bland. The deployment of the army pleased Cumberland and he made a short speech in which he implored his soldiers to defend King, country, religion, liberties and properties. The Royal lines then moved forward with fixed bayonets and came to a halt. Seeing this, one French officer told the Prince that he feared the outcome of the battle already determined for he had never seen men advance in so cool and regular manner. A similarly despondent Murray asked by Elcho about the day's prospects replied, 'We are putting an end to a bad affair.'

By one o'clock the opposing armies had taken up their respective positions and were at the ready. Charles had barely 5,000 men in all but expected the arrival of 2,000 absentees at any time. The Jacobite lines, facing east across the moor, were hopelessly askew prior to the battle, varying in distance from the English lines anything from between three and five hundred yards. They were also hemmed in between park walls on each flank, and as the wall on the left ended well before the wall on the right, the slanting was even greater. Lord George Murray had requested time to view the ground, but the impatient Prince had overruled him. Both men had failed to notice that the ground between their army and Cumberland's was considerably boggy and would make bad going for charging men. Murray's request to break down the western walls of the Culloden enclosures so as to

◀*Top: A contemporary painting of the battle by an unknown artist. The general background is identical with an engraving by Overton, but the artist has superimposed a larger-than-life equestrian portrait of the Duke of Cumberland. Near the feet of the Duke's horse is a discarded French standard, another exaggerated allusion to the presence of the French. As in other contemporary portrayals, the artist has included all the incidents of the battle. (Formerly Anne S. K. Brown Military Collection, Brown University)*

◀*A mid-nineteenth century image of the battle from Ballou's Pictorial. During the battle Charles was mounted on a newly acquired horse which, at the opening of the bombardment, was hit in the flank. The Prince dismounted and found another horse. Despite the impression given here, Charles in fact spent most of the battle on a small hill near a gap in the centre of the second line. (Anne S. K. Brown Military Collection, Brown University)*

allow the Athollmen to charge unimpeded was similarly rejected. The order of battle was arranged by Murray's bugbear, the Irishman O'Sullivan, who caused some dissent by refusing to allow the Camerons their traditional place at the right of the line. The choice of ground – a level, open stretch of moorland ideally suited for the movement of cavalry – was also O'Sullivan's.

From left to right the front line of the Jacobite army, stretched for 700 yards between two enclosure walls although many clansmen were still arriving on the field. The centre of the front line was commanded by Lord John Drummond, with the Duke of Perth commanding the left and Lord George Murray the right. The second line of the Prince's force was some seventy yards behind. Bringing up the rear were the few mounted troops of the Jacobite army. In all, the army was about 5,000 strong, but to many a trained eye it was obvious that the Jacobite army was in a hopeless situation as it faced the ordered lines of Royalist

▲*An engraving of Lord George Murray (1694-1760) after the painting by Jeremiah Davison. Murray fought at Prestonpans and Falkirk and successfully besieged his former home, Blair Castle, in March 1746. Although conventional, he was one of the finest of the Jacobite generals, but was frequently overruled by Prince Charles who favoured O'Sullivan. At Culloden he fought bravely, losing a horse and receiving several broadsword cuts to his coat. (Anne S. K. Brown Military Collection, Brown University)*

▶*'A Sketch of the Field of Battle at Culloden' by Thomas Sandby, 1746. Cumberland's 'official artist' witnessed the battle and recorded this accurate scene looking down the lines from high ground near Culloden Park with Highlanders attacking Barrell's Regiment in the far distance, and the disorderly movements in the centre. In the right foreground the Macdonalds are in position against the south-east corner of the enclosure wall. (Reproduced by gracious permission of Her Majesty the Queen)*

soldiers across the moor.

Some Highland officers feared a flanking movement on their right and left and suggested lining the walls with men, but their fears were quashed by the optimistic O'Sullivan. Charles shared his optimism, particularly when he observed that some of the Royal troops were having trouble deploying around the marshy ground on the right and left. For a few minutes the right wing of Cumberland's army was exposed as it attempted to negotiate the boggy ground and seeing this opportunity the Prince sent a message to Murray to move against the enemy, but for some unknown reason the Scottish lord did not comply. Possibly Murray felt that he had insufficient troops to make the attack; many Jacobites were only now arriving on the field. More probably Murray wanted Cumberland's front line to advance to the Leanach enclosures before he attacked.

Having stood for some time with rain and wind whipping their faces, the tired and hungry High-landers were in no mood to fight the 8,000 Redcoats and several hundred Argyll militia arrayed in three lines facing them across the several hundred yards of open moorland.

## The Opening Cannonade

Having halted his army and retrieved the artillery which had been bogged down, the Duke called up his 3-pounders and placed them in pairs between the six front-line regiments. Six Coehorn mortars were deployed in two batteries slightly ahead of the two regiments on the wings of the second line. In comparison the Jacobite artillery strength was insignificant: twelve guns of various calibre, ranging from 1- to 4-pounders, were deployed in three 4-gun batteries in the centre and on the wings of the front line.

Much to Charles's displeasure, the Royal army showed no sign of advancing and anxiety swept through the eager Highlanders. Shortly after one

o'clock, under rain showers, someone in the Prince's army – possibly the Master of Ordnance, John Finlayson – ordered the few inexperienced gunners manning the batteries to fire on the red lines. Apparently the Prince's artillerymen were provoked by the appearance of Lord Bury, the son of Lord Albemarle, within 100 yards of the Highlanders. He had emerged from the dead ground between the two armies after an un-successful reconnaissance of the rebel battery positions, and returned to the ranks of his cheering countrymen as the first shot from the Jacobite centre battery sailed over his head and killed a soldier in the rear. The round had been deliberately ranged on the rear ranks where the Duke was thought to be. A second shot from the battery on the left wing narrowly missed the conspicuous, 18-stone Cumberland, astride his large grey horse,

▲ 'The Battle of Culloden' by Lionel Edwards. This retrospective illustration depicts Pulteney's Regiment deployed in three ranks on the extreme right of the Duke's front line, presenting volley fire to the Macdonalds who are reluctant to continue their advance. Standing behind the soldiers are sergeants, with officers behind them and on the flanks. The mounted figure in the right middle distance is a major of Kingston's Horse, advancing to outflank the Jacobites. (Anne S. K. Brown Military Collection, Brown University)

▲ Argyll Militia (or Campbell Militiamen) who were detested by the clansmen of the Jacobite army. They wore basically the same dress as that of the Prince's supporters, especially the belted plaid, although originally it had been intended to provide a short red coat. The complement of weapons would have been similar also. (Anne S. K. Brown Military Collection, Brown University)

but killed two men in front of him. The High-landers gave a loud shout and waved their bonnets at the sound of this first discharge of the Prince's cannon. Some of the Duke's dragoons had diffi-culty with their horses, nervous from the noise, but soon recovered their poise.

Two minutes later the sixteen 3-pounders of the Royal artillery belched out their first deadly missiles. It had been an effort to haul the bogged guns on to firmer ground, but now they were ready and were opening up on the exposed Jacobite line, some 300 yards away. In command of the guns was

# The Battle of Culloden, 16 April 1746: Initial Dispositions

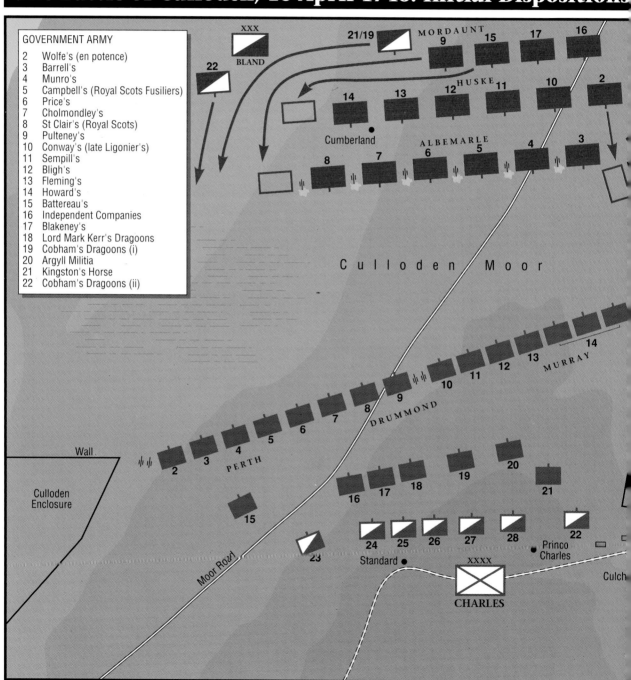

GOVERNMENT ARMY

2 Wolfe's (en potence)
3 Barrell's
4 Munro's
5 Campbell's (Royal Scots Fusiliers)
6 Price's
7 Cholmondley's
8 St Clair's (Royal Scots)
9 Pulteney's
10 Conway's (late Ligonier's)
11 Sempill's
12 Bligh's
13 Fleming's
14 Howard's
15 Battereau's
16 Independent Companies
17 Blakeney's
18 Lord Mark Kerr's Dragoons
19 Cobham's Dragoons (i)
20 Argyll Militia
21 Kingston's Horse
22 Cobham's Dragoons (ii)

Brevet-Colonel William Belford who, having spotted a group of horsemen in the rebel rear through his glass, directed fire in the hope of killing the Prince himself. Charles was unscathed, but a number of men including his groom and some of his hussars were killed. This was the first time from the outset of the campaign that the Highlanders had been exposed to artillery fire – it had been virtually absent at Prestonpans and Falkirk – and the swirling smoke and the round shot ploughing through their ranks was disconcerting in the extreme. The Jacobite guns responded feebly. Unable to find their targets, within nine minutes most had fallen silent, many of the gunners having fled as soon as the Royal artillery began firing. The smoke from the Royal guns also made it impossible for the Jacobite gunners to range their weapons, although one gun had been dragged to the south-east corner of the enclosure and was still firing. The English cannonade continued relentlessly and more Highlanders fell, but still the order to advance – 'Claymore!' – did not come, only the shouts of 'Close-up! Close-up!' as more and more gaps appeared in the ragged lines. It is thought that most of the Prince's casualties were suffered during this bombardment.

The Royal gunners were still trying to locate Charles who was near his standard under the protection of Kilmarnock's dismounted troopers behind the centre of the second line. Urged to move towards the right wing away from the carnage, he stationed himself on a small hillock near Culchunaig, guarded by Balmerino's Life Guards and sixteen troopers from Fitz-James's Horse. In this ill-chosen position, remote from his troops, the nature of the ground and the bad weather prevented him from seeing clearly the unfolding situation. In sole command for the first time, he was so far removed as to be completely ineffectual. His bewilderment at seeing so many of his men cut down and his frustration at the English delay in attacking left him unable to decide what to do next. Watching the destruction with expectant admiration and pride, the men in the English ranks stood still and waited, growing in confidence minute by minute. The wind was at their backs and they could see the smoke blinding and confusing the Highlanders. Cumberland was content to save his infantry and let his guns do the work for them, but he felt sure that the Highlanders' advance would not be long delayed. Accordingly he made some changes to the deployment of his troops by moving Pulteney's Regiment from the rear to the right of the front rank in order to counter the

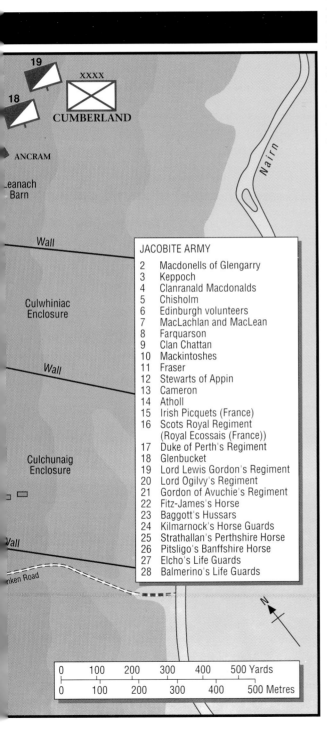

19
18
XXXX
CUMBERLAND

ANCRAM

Leanach Barn

Nairn

Wall

Culwhiniac Enclosure

Wall

Culchunaig Enclosure

Wall

nken Road

N

JACOBITE ARMY

2   Macdonells of Glengarry
3   Keppoch
4   Clanranald Macdonalds
5   Chisholm
6   Edinburgh volunteers
7   MacLachlan and MacLean
8   Farquarson
9   Clan Chattan
10  Mackintoshes
11  Fraser
12  Stewarts of Appin
13  Cameron
14  Atholl
15  Irish Picquets (France)
16  Scots Royal Regiment
    (Royal Ecossais (France))
17  Duke of Perth's Regiment
18  Glenbucket
19  Lord Lewis Gordon's Regiment
20  Lord Ogilvy's Regiment
21  Gordon of Avuchie's Regiment
22  Fitz-James's Horse
23  Baggott's Hussars
24  Kilmarnock's Horse Guards
25  Strathallan's Perthshire Horse
26  Pitsligo's Banffshire Horse
27  Elcho's Life Guards
28  Balmerino's Life Guards

| 0 | 100 | 200 | 300 | 400 | 500 Yards |
| 0 | 100 | 200 | 300 | 400 | 500 Metres |

◄ *'William Barrell' by Thomas Hudson. This portrait was painted three years after Culloden, and shortly before Barrell's death and burial in Westminster Abbey in 1749. Formerly an adjutant in the Regiment of Guards, Barrell developed a system of drill which entailed waving the Colours in eight distinctive flourishes. When he assumed command of the 4th Foot in 1734 the drill was adopted and subsequently by many other regiments. At Culloden, Barrell's Regiment was commanded by Lieutenant-Colonel Rich. (Anne S. K. Brown Military Collection, Brown University)*

Macdonalds who outflanked the Royal troops. Battereau's men were also brought up from the rear to the second line to fill the right-hand flank should Pulteney's soldiers give way. Thinking that he would not need a reserve, the Duke left a token regiment, Blakeney's, in the rear. Kingston's 200 troopers, joined shortly after by 60 of Cobham's mounted men, were also moved to the right of Pulteney's to prepare for a flanking attack.

Murray had considered a flanking movement against Cumberland on the latter's left wing near the Culwhiniac enclosure, but the Duke had been quick to realize the threat, feeling that it was there that the balance of the battle would lie. Accordingly, a contingent of Wolfe's Regiment under Major-General John Huske was moved to a position at right angles *en potence* to Barrell's men on the extreme left of the Duke's front line. Here, with their backs to a stone dike wall, they faced down the Royal front rank to enfilade the imminent Highlanders' charge with rapid musketry. The remainder of Cobham's cavalry, 240 men in all, had now linked up with Lord Mark Kerr's 300 troopers to the left of the Leanach barn near the

▶'William Blakeney' (1672-1761), painted by Chalmers in Minorca in 1755. He was commanding the garrison at Stirling Castle when it was unsuccessfully besieged by the Highlanders. He ordered a sally against the siege works which cost the enemy 300 dead. At Culloden his Regiment was in reserve and was not called upon. Having proved himself at Stirling Castle and in view of his popularity among the troops, Blakeney was sent to Minorca where, in 1756, he gallantly defended the fortress against the French for 70 days before being forced to surrender. (Anne S. K. Brown Military Collection, Brown University)

loyalist Argyll Militia and were awaiting further orders. Cumberland himself had ridden to a position towards the right of the second line in front of Howard's Regiment in anticipation of a flanking movement in that direction from the Macdonalds. Two lines of Redcoats now awaited the next phase of the battle: Cobham's and Kingston's cavalry, Pulteney's, the Royals (St. Clair's), Cholmondeley's, Price's, the Royal Scots Fusiliers (Campbell's), Munro's, and Barrell's, with Wolfe's troops at right angles. A few dozen yards behind them stood the second line of Battereau's, Howard's, Fleming's, Bligh's, Sempill's and Ligonier's Regiments deployed right to left. In the rear towards the left stood Blakeney's Regiment. The extreme left wing was held by the cavalry under Kerr, and the Argyll Militia.

## The Highlanders' Charge

The firing continued to cut large swathes through the rebel lines for upwards of twenty minutes, although some accounts estimate the duration of the cannonade at anything from nine to 30

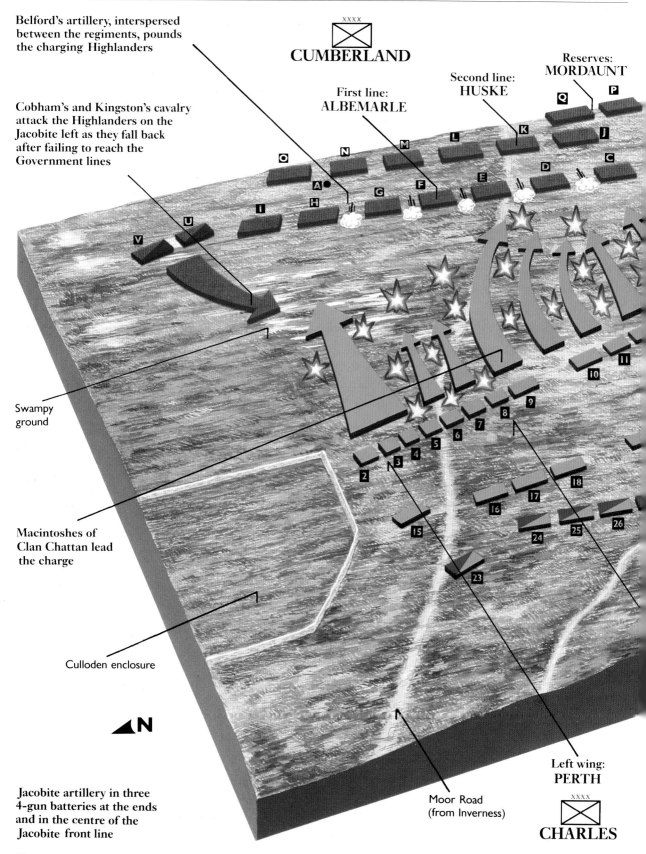

Belford's artillery, interspersed between the regiments, pounds the charging Highlanders

Cobham's and Kingston's cavalry attack the Highlanders on the Jacobite left as they fall back after failing to reach the Government lines

XXXX
CUMBERLAND

Reserves:
MORDAUNT

Second line:
HUSKE

First line:
ALBEMARLE

Swampy ground

Macintoshes of Clan Chattan lead the charge

Culloden enclosure

N

Jacobite artillery in three 4-gun batteries at the ends and in the centre of the Jacobite front line

Moor Road (from Inverness)

Left wing:
PERTH

XXXX
CHARLES

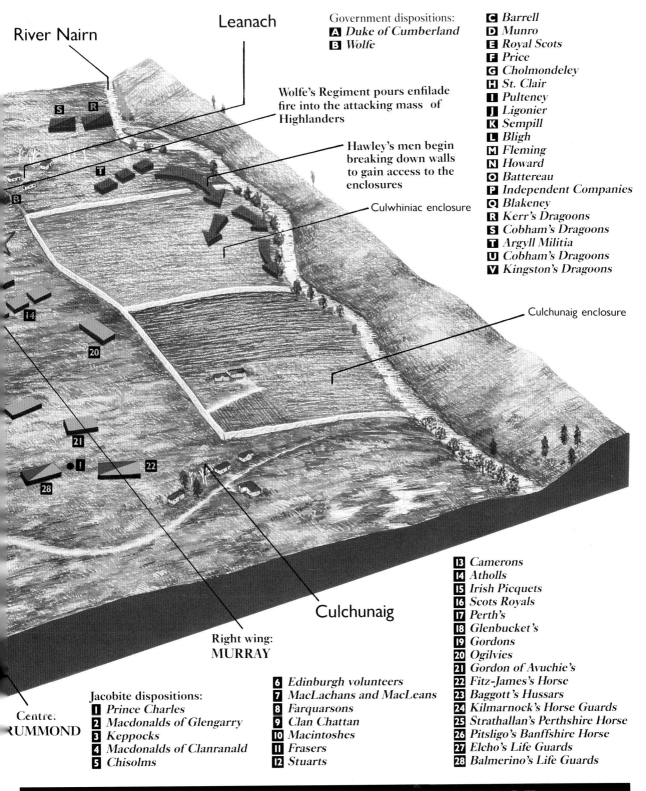

River Nairn

Leanach

Government dispositions:
**A** *Duke of Cumberland*
**B** *Wolfe*

**C** *Barrell*
**D** *Munro*
**E** *Royal Scots*
**F** *Price*
**G** *Cholmondeley*
**H** *St. Clair*
**I** *Pulteney*
**J** *Ligonier*
**K** *Sempill*
**L** *Bligh*
**M** *Fleming*
**N** *Howard*
**O** *Battereau*
**P** *Independent Companies*
**Q** *Blakeney*
**R** *Kerr's Dragoons*
**S** *Cobham's Dragoons*
**T** *Argyll Militia*
**U** *Cobham's Dragoons*
**V** *Kingston's Dragoons*

Wolfe's Regiment pours enfilade fire into the attacking mass of Highlanders

Hawley's men begin breaking down walls to gain access to the enclosures

Culwhiniac enclosure

Culchunaig enclosure

Culchunaig

Right wing: MURRAY

Centre: RUMMOND

**13** *Camerons*
**14** *Atholls*
**15** *Irish Picquets*
**16** *Scots Royals*
**17** *Perth's*
**18** *Glenbucket's*
**19** *Gordons*
**20** *Ogilvies*
**21** *Gordon of Avuchie's*
**22** *Fitz-James's Horse*
**23** *Baggott's Hussars*
**24** *Kilmarnock's Horse Guards*
**25** *Strathallan's Perthshire Horse*
**26** *Pitsligo's Banffshire Horse*
**27** *Elcho's Life Guards*
**28** *Balmerino's Life Guards*

Jacobite dispositions:
**1** *Prince Charles*
**2** *Macdonalds of Glengarry*
**3** *Keppocks*
**4** *Macdonalds of Clanranald*
**5** *Chisolms*
**6** *Edinburgh volunteers*
**7** *MacLachans and MacLeans*
**8** *Farquarsons*
**9** *Clan Chattan*
**10** *Macintoshes*
**11** *Frasers*
**12** *Stuarts*

# CULLODEN: THE HIGHLANDERS' CHARGE

**Shortly after 1.30 p.m. 16 April 1746, as seen from the west**

minutes. Belford now changed from shot to grape in the hope of finishing off the enemy. The result was devastating: more and more of the Highlanders in their tightly packed ranks, swelled by men arriving on the field, collapsed dead or wounded under a withering hailstorm of lead pellets from the Royal artillery's front-line guns. Some deliberately fell to the ground to protect themselves; others fled in fear. It was now obvious to O'Sullivan that the army, being weaker in artillery, must charge. For practical purposes his artillery now consisted of a single gun on the right wing and an additional gun which had been brought up by a French engineer to a position at the south-east corner of the enclosure wall.

Shortly before 1.30 p.m., with a squall of hail and rain lashing the clansmen, the order to charge was given. Lord George Murray, who described the regiments in the front rank as 'so impatient that they were like to break their ranks', had been approached by several clan leaders anxious for a decision and fearful that they would be unable to hold their men much longer amidst the terrible slaughter. The restive Mackintoshes urged their leader, Lochiel, to persuade Murray to order the charge. Murray sent Kerr of Graden to the Prince who consented to the attack. By now the Jacobite line was skewed, the right wing being well in

▲Standard-bearer of a Highland militia company carrying a standard of George II's; a contemporary engraving by Engelbrecht. While most of the Royal regiments bore regimental standards, other flags were also carried. One which appears in the scene of the crossing of the Spey bears the cipher 'GR' as in this illustration. The Jacobite standards are unknown, but English engravers occasionally represented French flags and a strange device on Charles's standard of a coffin surmounted by a crown. (Anne S. K. Brown Military Collection, Brown University)

▲David Morier's famous painting of the battle, which was probably painted for the Duke of Cumberland. The scene depicts the close encounter between Barrell's Regiment and elements of the Jacobite left wing. The uniforms of the Royal soldiers are accurate; the eight clansmen are wearing garments in more than twenty ancient tartans. Morier used Highland prisoners taken at the battle for his models. The artist painted several portraits of Cumberland in Scotland. (Reproduced by gracious permission of Her Majesty the Queen)

advance of the left, so Kerr directed the Duke of Perth on the left to move to the attack. Laclan MacLachan, one of Charles's aides-de-camp, was sent to Murray, who was with the Athollmen on the right, to order the attack, but was killed by round shot before he got to the front. Further delay ensued, while more and more casualties were sustained. Charles then sent Sir John Macdonald to the left and Brigadier Stapleton to the right with orders for the line to advance. The order was received, but the Macdonalds refused and were urged on only a few paces level with the other regiments in the front line.

Some of the Highlanders could wait no longer. In rage and despair the Mackintoshes of the Clan Chattan in the centre 'scrugged' their bonnets over their heads, broke the ragged line and darted forward through the wet heather, spurred-on by

◀ *'George Howard', by Reynolds. At Culloden Lieutenant- Colonel Howard (1720-96) commanded the 3rd Foot (Buffs) which, with Batterau's Regiment, formed the right wing of Cumberland's second line. He had also led the Regiment at Fontenoy and Falkirk. Howard was in danger of losing his life when attacked by Lord Strathallan, but managed to run his sword through the Scotsman. One source has it that Howard '. . . merited everlasting execration by his treatment of those to whom Lord Loudoun had promised indemnity after Culloden'. (Anne S. K. Brown Military Collection, Brown University)*

the pipes and by their commander, the yellow-haired Colonel MacGillivray. Grape-shot continued to pepper the oncoming clansmen. At their heels came the men of Atholl and the Camerons who had been positioned on the right of the Clan Chattan, but the direction of their charge changed suddenly towards the left to avoid some walls and towards the firmer ground of an old moor road. At the same time, the Macintoshes veered right to avoid the boggy ground between the two armies, and possibly forced by the heavy musketry which opened up from the centre of the Royal ranks. Confused and blinded by smoke, many were lost in the mêlée, or fell to the brisk firing from the Royal centre. Survivors later stated that they were caught in thick smoke and became disorientated. The Clan Chattan lost eighteen officers and hundreds of men before getting within twenty yards of the Royal lines. Similarly, the Athollmen were cut down before they had a chance to engage.

▶*A Highland officer as depicted in a mid-18th century engraving by Martin Engelbrecht. The artist depicted several Highland soldiers who served in the various wars in Europe from about 1745-1763, but it is not known what sources he used. The costume is basically correct although a little romanticized. (Anne S. K. Brown Military Collection)*

They had run broadsides to Wolfe's men lining the wall who decimated them with accurate musket fire. The walls on each flank had a funnelling effect, forcing the charging clansmen into an area little more than 300 yards wide. Undeterred, the dense mass now crammed into this narrow corridor against the park wall and the Leanach dike, and moved towards the left of the Duke's army to engage the men of Barrell's, Munro's and Wolfe's Regiments. In the few seconds it took to cover the distance, many of the Highlanders, unable to fire their customary volley because of the congestion, discarded their primed muskets and pistols and resorted to the broadsword, scythe blades or axes. For a moment the Prince's soldiers were shrouded in cannon smoke, but as it lifted they saw an orderly line of Redcoats, 30 yards away, who levelled their muskets and fired an accurate and deadly volley; a distinctive counterpoint to the monotonous pounding of Belford's guns which continued to fire. The troops in the front rank knelt to fire while two other ranks stood behind with muskets raised to shoulder, to providing continuous firing as one line after another reloaded. The enfilade fire from Wolfe's men in front of the Leanach dike was now beginning to take effect, but the shouting Highlanders came on pell-mell towards the left.

Seeing the pressure on his left wing, Cumberland ordered some of the regiments in the second line to move 50 yards to the left in anticipation of a breakthrough by the Highlanders which was not long in coming. The men of Barrell's and Munro's, having had time for only one volley, raised their muskets with fixed bayonets to meet the onslaught of 1,500 Highlanders who crashed into them full tilt. Many of the English soldiers were seriously wounded including Lord Robert Kerr and Lieutenant-Colonel Rich. According to one account, 'The Highlanders fought like furies and Barrell's behaved like so many heroes.' As the clansmen created a wedge that forced Barrell's 350 men outwards to form on Sempill's, they came to grief on the bayonets of Sempill's and Bligh's Regiments. A soldier of the Royal army wrote, 'Our lads fought more like devils than men. In short we laid . . . about 1,600 dead on the spot . . .'

Sempill's troops were filling the gap behind Barrell's and Munro's men and upon them fell the brunt of the Highlanders' attack but due to the closeness of the English front ranks, many of Sempill's men could not fire with accuracy and a number of Barrell's men may have been shot by their own side. None the less, the English firing was deadly and those clansmen who were not felled by bullets were stopped by the bayonet. 'Give them the bayonet!' was the command. Cumberland's training was paying off. As one Royal officer claimed, the directions 'made an essential difference, staggered the enemy who was not prepared to alter their way of fighting, and destroyed them in a manner rather to be conceived than told'.

The charge petered out with straggling groups of Highlanders running senselessly this way and that between the two lines of Royal troops seeking a way out. A soldier of Cumberland's army recalled the scene: 'About 500 Jacobites penetrated the Royal lines. They were forced through our front Line, they were now between two Lines, and our Front completing again, they were severely handled both Ways: for those who escaped the fire of Bligh's and Sempill's Regiments met a worse Destruction from the Bayonets of our first Line, there being scarce one Soldier in Barrell's Regiment who did not each kill several Men . . .' Few of those who broke through the English lines survived to tell the tale. Lochiel, wounded in both ankles, was carried from the field by two Highlanders while his forlorn Camerons disengaged and began to retreat. In desperation, others threw stones at the Redcoats which amused Cumberland. Those who broke back from the line were swept by Wolfe's muskets and by mortar shells and grape-shot. Lord George Murray had also ridden through the English lines and having been thrown by his horse managed to fight his way back to his men on foot. Realizing that the crisis was upon them, he tried to encourage the second line of Highlanders and some French troops, but it was clear that all was lost.

Towards the centre and left, the Highlanders were faring little better. The advance of the Clan Chattan and others on the right had inspired others to follow. The MacLeans and MacLachlans charged, but – the rebel line being skewed – they had further open ground to cover and none reached the Royal lines; the musket fire from the Royals and Pulteney's was so deadly that no living thing could survive. Of the 200 MacLeans, whose boast it was that they never gave ground, 150 were killed. Keppoch and Macdonnell of Scothouse died in the thick of the action, the latter only twenty paces from the enemy. The dead ground between the two armies was littered with dead and dying clansmen. Less enthusiastic were the Farquharsons and the Macdonalds. Since early morning the Macdonalds of the Glengarry Regiment had been complaining about their placement on the extreme left of the Jacobite line, and the Duke of Perth had tried to placate them. When the Regiment saw the Highlanders' charge on the right and centre they advanced a few paces and began to run towards the Royal lines, firing pistols and waving their swords in the vain hope of tempting the Royal troops to attack. Some fell into

▲ *A Victorian impression of the battle by R. R. McIan, inspired by Morier's painting, and exhibited in 1853. In the foreground men are engaged at close quarters while in the middle distance fire from the Royal troops is thinning the ranks of the enemy. Barrell's Regiment, which bore the brunt of the Highland charge, lost eighteen men killed and 108 wounded at Culloden. (Anne S. K. Brown Military Collection, Brown University)*

▶ *David Wemyss, Lord Elcho (1721-87) who laid the groundwork for the Rebellion with a visit to Scotland in 1744. Initially opposed to the plan, he threw his support behind Prince Charles and, after Prestonpans, raised a force of about 100 gentlemen as Life Guards. It was they who formed up on the right flank to oppose the Royal dragoons and helped cover the retreat of the Jacobite right wing. Elcho accompanied Charles from the field and dissuaded him from any further efforts to rally his supporters. (Anne S. K. Brown Military Collection, Brown University)*

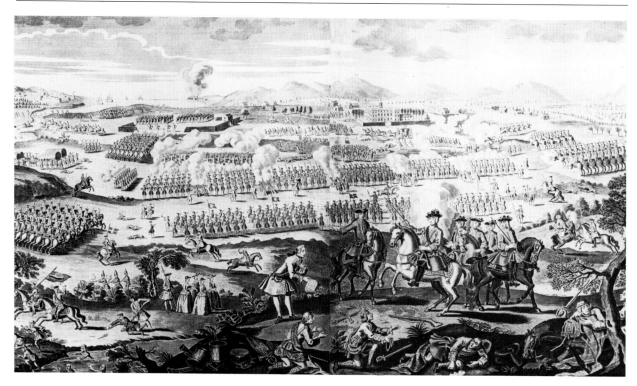

◄A highly imaginative impression of the battle, intended purely as an illustration but represented in the manner typical of eighteenth-century military pictures with the commanding general on a rearing white horse in the foreground. Cumberland would never have placed himself in such a vulnerable position nor, contrary to popular myth, did he watch the battle from a huge boulder at the eastern edge of the battlefield. He spent most of the time astride his horse riding casually towards the right of the second line regiments. (Reproduced with permission from Aberdeen University Library)

◀ 'A Representation of the Battle on Drummossie Moor near Culloden' as depicted in a contemporary print by Henry Overton, published two months after the battle. All the main incidents of the battle are shown, but with several anachronisms – the explosion at Fort Augustus, and four Jacobite ladies who were arrested later at Inverness. The main figure to the left of Cumberland is a French officer offering his surrender. In fact, 222 French soldiers were captured, but it is doubtful if Cumberland received their surrender. (Courtesy of the Director, National Army Museum, London)

▶ A contemporary view of a Highlander by the Austrian artist Martin Engelbrecht, published in Augsburg. This was the typical Continental view of Highland Scots of the mid-18th century, although the artist has depicted plaid trews rather than the kilt and the design on the targe is purely fanciful. (Anne S. K. Brown Military Collection)

knee-deep water and could advance no further because of the swampy ground. They were swept by musket fire, it being said by Cumberland that his infantry 'hardly took their firelocks from their shoulders' and, seeing activity amongst the Royal cavalry suggesting a flanking movement, started to retrace their steps, just as other clans in their rear began to flee the field. Some officers charged with Keppoch, but many including the leader were felled by musket balls. A number of the Macdonalds were brought off by picquets before they could be surrounded by Kingston's Horse. The guns of the Royal artillery continued to fire relentlessly and stragglers were still being killed by grape-shot. To add to the slaughter Cobham's 60 troopers and Kingston's Horse moved off from the Royal lines and rode in amongst the fugitives, hacking at them without mercy. The Jacobite lines were in complete disarray, with gaps left by the fleeing clansmen. The battle had been raging for less than half-an-hour, but the left and centre of the army no longer existed.

## The Cavalry Attacks on the Flanks

At the outset of the bombardment, the Campbells of the Argyll Militia were seen to detach themselves from the Duke's army and move towards the enclosed lands around Culwhiniac between the river and the Jacobite army in order to outflank the Athollmen. In fact, the situation of the Culwhiniac enclosure had been ignored by all the Prince's officers except Murray who had wanted to remove the walls. John O'Sullivan had commented: 'Never fear, my Lord, they can't come between you and the river unless they break the walls of these two parks that are between you and them.' It had been O'Sullivan's feeling that having walls on each flank of the army would guard against encirclement. He had failed to observe the obvious – that walls have

◀Henry Hawley (c. 1679-1759) commanded the Royal cavalry at Falkirk and Culloden, having also served at Dettingen and Fontenoy. He was almost censured for his handling of the army at Falkirk, but his replacement, Cumberland, admired Hawley's harsh methods of restoring discipline, with frequent resort to capital punishment, and he was given overall command of the cavalry and the various militia units at Culloden. Many of the excesses committed by his troopers after the battle were at 'Hangman' Hawley's orders. (Society for Army Historical Research)

gates, and that the enclosure of Culwhiniac could be by-passed by troops to take the Highland army in the rear. The Duke of Perth wanted to line the walls but Lord George Murray did not have enough soldiers to garrison the enclosures. As an afterthought Ogilvy's Regiment was sent to guard the flank. When two officers were sent to observe the movements in the enclosures – and indeed sighted some dragoons at the far end, they reported back that the river banks were too high to allow mounted troops to approach from that direction unless they broke down the walls. Murray was now concerned about the presence of the Royal dragoons and ordered Ogilvy to keep a close watch on the position. At the same time O'Sullivan took a hundred men to the north side of the dike.

From the river to the moor, between farms and the East Park of the Culwhiniac farm, ran a sunken lane and here five squadrons of His Majesty's cavalry were biding their time. The Argyll Militiamen armed with axes made a breach at the corner

▶'*Lieutenant-General Sir John Ligonier'(1680-1770), by Worsdale. Having distinguished himself at Dettingen, he served as adviser to the young Cumberland at Fontenoy. When the Rising broke out he led the forces in Lancashire but was back in London at the time of Culloden. His younger brother, Francis, was in command of a regiment during the Rebellion but was ill prior to Falkirk; however, he left his sickbed to rally the dragoons at the battle but died shortly afterwards. At Culloden his Regiment was commanded by Henry Seymour Conway who succeeded to the colonelcy only ten days before the battle. (Anne S. K. Brown Military Collection, Brown University)*

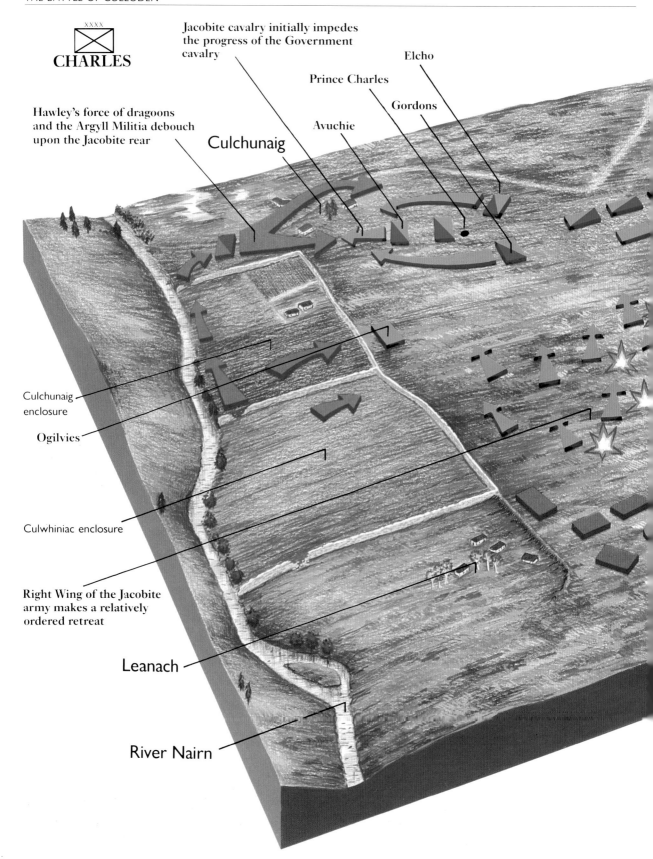

CHARLES

Jacobite cavalry initially impedes the progress of the Government cavalry

Elcho

Prince Charles

Gordons

Avuchie

Hawley's force of dragoons and the Argyll Militia debouch upon the Jacobite rear

Culchunaig

Culchunaig enclosure

Ogilvies

Culwhiniac enclosure

Right Wing of the Jacobite army makes a relatively ordered retreat

Leanach

River Nairn

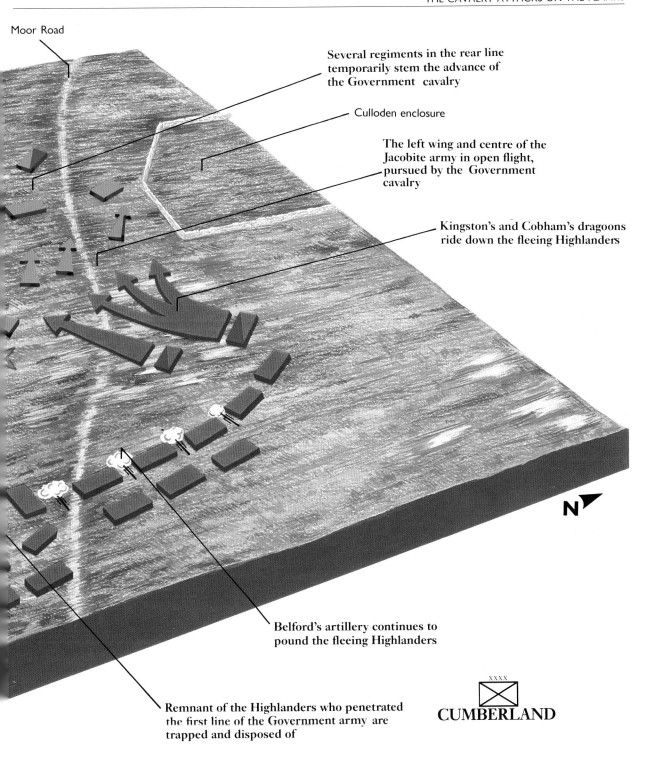

Moor Road

Several regiments in the rear line
temporarily stem the advance of
the Government cavalry

Culloden enclosure

The left wing and centre of the
Jacobite army in open flight,
pursued by the Government
cavalry

Kingston's and Cobham's dragoons
ride down the fleeing Highlanders

Belford's artillery continues to
pound the fleeing Highlanders

Remnant of the Highlanders who penetrated
the first line of the Government army are
trapped and disposed of

XXXX
CUMBERLAND

N

# CULLODEN: THE ROYALIST ATTACK
## Mid-afternoon 16 April 1746, as seen from the east

FIRTH OF MURRAY

▲ 'A Perspective View of the Glorious Battle' after J. Hamilton, published in 1746. Many in England regarded the Rising as French inspired and so many contemporary engravings played heavily on this theme. In this example a grinning grenadier retrieves a French standard from the pool in the foreground. Other scenes include women stripping bodies, four prisoners, and the loyalist Captain John Campbell of Sempill's Regiment holding a spontoon. Campbell was sent to take possession of Inverness after the battle. (Courtesy of the Director, National Army Museum, London)

◀MacBean, wearing the tartan of the MacIntoshes, fighting off the English in a romantic illustration by R. R. McIan. When the Argyll Militia broke down the wall to attack the flank, Major Gillies MacBean stood at the gap with his broadsword. As the enemy came through he cut thirteen of them down including Lord Robert Kerr. He was eventually surrounded and, despite the pleas of an officer to 'save that brave man', Macbean fell from several bayonet wounds and musket balls. (Anne S. K. Brown Military Collection, Brown University)

▶Cumberland's Light Dragoons, after a painting by David Morier. The regiment was raised in autumn 1746 from members of Kingston's Light Horse, a unit that had been raised to meet the Jacobite threat in 1745 and served on the right wing of the Government army at Culloden. Fourteen officers from Kingston's Horse transferred into the new regiment, which went on to serve in Flanders in 1747. (Anne S. Brown Military Collection).

of the walls beside the river and ran westwards along the farthest dike by the Water of Nairn. Another group moved northwards inside the wall which ran parallel with the sunken road. A third group and some dragoons advanced across the East Park of Culwhiniac and it was they who were seen by the Jacobites. Coming to a wall separating the East Park from the West, a second breach was made. To counter the flanking movement, Murray moved Gordon of Avochie's Battalion in the direction of the Argyll Militia and brought up Fitz-James's Horse to face the threat from the Duke's cavalry. Some Campbells began to fire upon the fleeing Jacobites, particularly the Camerons, and charged out of the park with raised swords, losing half-a-dozen men and two officers in the process. Cobham's and Kerr's dragoons, about 500 well-armed and disciplined troopers in ten squadrons,

led by Hawley, having gained access through the torn down walls began the flanking movement on the left. Some opposition was encountered from clansmen of Avochie's Battalion, but they were soon dispersed and the dragoons moved into position near some houses at Culchunaig. In fact, Murray later stated that the enemy approached without being fired on by Ogilvy's Regiment who were originally lining the wall, but who for some unknown reason had been withdrawn to form a reserve with orders not to fire unless directed to do so. Misunderstanding or not, it was probably the worst single order of the entire battle and allowed the Royal cavalry to outflank the Jacobite right wing virtually unmolested.

The Prince's cavalry of Elcho's Life Guards and Fitz-James's Horse formed up to oppose the Royal threat in the enclosures. This dishevelled remnant of about 160 men, from an original contingent of 400 troopers, riding tired and hungry mounts, were unable to charge because of the boggy ground, but they plunged into the Royal cavalry as it moved along the sunken road, inflicting some losses with pistol and carbine fire. But they were no match for trained cavalrymen. It would have been easy enough for the Royal cavalry to remove this threat, but they were reluctant to press on, preferring instead to advance at a slow pace. It had been a vain attempt but it nevertheless provided valuable time for the Prince's right wing to make an orderly retreat. In fact, for ten vital minutes, the Jacobite cavalry under Lord Elcho and Colonel O'Shea delayed the Royal cavalry from gaining access to the moor where they could have massacred the fleeing Highlanders. When Hawley's men did break out, Fitz-James's Horse retreated to form a protective square around their fleeing comrades. The Prince's other cavalry, the

▼'An Exact View of the Glorious Victory', published in October 1746 by Bakewell. All the principal events of the battle are represented and in the distance can be seen Fort George above Inverness. The dragoons are well through the gaps in the walls and are engaging Jacobite cavalry, while in the foreground a French officer surrenders his sword to Cumberland. Other vignettes include the Jacobite baggage train, a wounded soldier and the Royalist baggage guarded by Militiamen. (Courtesy of the Director, National Army Museum, London)

Perthshire Horse and some hussars, failed to attack but one of their leaders, Lord Strathallan, charged headlong towards some English troops but was killed instantly by Colonel Howard.

The right wing of the Highland army was now making a hasty retreat in an orderly fashion considering the circumstances. Credit must be given to Lord George Murray and Lord Ogilvy with two battalions of Angus men. Like Fitz-James's Horse, they organized themselves into a square formation, frequently turning round to fend off Royal troopers. Legend has it that on one occasion during the retreat some clansmen were confronted by a party of Royal cavalry who moved out of their way and allowed them to pass

unmolested. Certainly it was known that Hawley's cavalry were reluctant to attack Jacobites in formation, preferring instead to tackle the stragglers and wounded.

As Cobham's and Kerr's men moved on to the moor and commenced their butchery, the Jacobite left wing – in contrast to the right – was beginning its retreat in great disorder, harassed by Kingston's Horse who were moving round to meet up with the English cavalry from the left wing. They attacked the Royal Scots who had been in the centre of the Highland line while Cobham's cavalry attacked them from the rear. Fortunately for the Scots, the Irish Picquets prevented a complete encirclement with a steady fire, which saved almost one hundred lives, until they themselves were forced to seek cover behind a wall, before quitting the field for Inverness. The guns were still pounding away as Cumberland and his staff contented themselves with watching the ensuing slaughter.

Several hundred yards away, Prince Charles had observed the pending crisis in the enclosures, but had sent no reinforcements, and as his cavalry gave way, he was escorted away from the fray at the suggestion of O'Sullivan who, acknowledging that all was lost, exclaimed, 'Yu see all is going to pot. Yu can be of no great succor, so before a general deroute which will soon be, seize the Prince and take him off.' Charles was so far back that there was never any danger of being captured, but he left the field in the direction of Balvraid accompanied by the remnant of two Highland Regiments, Glenbucket's and John Roy Stewart's. Disillusioned at the sight of fleeing soldiers (probably from the left wing) whom he had thought invincible, he tried to persuade them to attempt one more charge, offering to dismount and lead them in person. 'Rally, in the name of God. Pray, gentlemen, return,' he shouted, but few paid heed to his urging, and his companions begged him to consider his own safety. Among the last to leave Drummossie Moor were the French and Irish troops. In just under one hour the flower of Scotland had been overwhelmingly crushed. With the exception of Lord Nairn, Murray and Charles Stuart Ardshiel, most of the Jacobite commanders were dead or wounded, and one-third of all the men from the regiments in the centre or right wing were dead. Indeed, of the men who had charged with the Mackintoshes, only three survived.

## The Pursuit

While Charles was making his way towards the ford of Faillie over the Nairn, the Royal cavalry from both wings were riding together all over Drummossie Moor, cutting at anything that moved before pursuing the fleeing Jacobites towards the road to Ruthven. At the ford Charles, who was 'in a deplorable state', convinced that treachery had lost the battle, met Elcho and O'Sullivan to plan the next move. The sight of more Jacobite officers fleeing made him even more despondent. It was decided to move towards Fraser country, but orders sent to Highland officers asking them to assemble at Ruthven were quickly changed, and they were told to disperse.

Meanwhile the fields around Culloden House were searched for fugitives by Kingston's troopers before they headed down the road to Inverness, chasing fleeing Highlanders and sabreing any who stood their ground. These cavalrymen were vengeful following an incident earlier in the month when they had been surprised by Jacobites at Keith. A participant described the present scene: 'Immediately our Horse that was on the right and left wings pursued them with sword and pistol and cut a great many of them down so I never saw a small field so thick with dead.' Many non-combatants were slaughtered including two weavers at Ballavrat, a blacksmith, and a father and son ploughing in a field. An estimated 1,500 Highlanders, having slept through the battle, came from cottages and fields to swell the rout. It was not long before the clatter of hooves on paving stones announced the arrival of the Royal cavalry. Dismounting, they demanded food and lodgings. The remnant of the Highland army, mostly those who had been on the right and centre of the line, moved off with colours flying and pipes playing towards Balvraid and on

◀Dragoons riding down Highlanders in a modern illustration. Given a free hand, the Royal troopers went berserk, hacking and sabreing anything that moved. The majority of the atrocities committed after the battle were by the Royal cavalry who outflanked the Jacobite forces and then pursued fugitives towards Inverness. (Anne S. K. Brown Military Collection, Brown University)

*1, Private of an Independent Highland Company: 2, Fusilier of the Royal Ecossais; 3, Trooper, Baggot's Hussars; 4, Sergeant, Irish Picquets. (G. A. Embleton)*

◀ 'Cumberland after Culloden', by John Wootton, published in 1747. A highly idealized portrayal of the Duke at the battle, clearly aimed at celebrating his victory in a popular print of the time. The anguish of the defeated Highlanders trodden underfoot and the broken weapons symbolize the power and supremacy of the Duke. While the background is purely fanciful, the artist has touched upon reality with the cavalry attack on the left flank and the Royal Navy ships in the Moray Firth. (Anne S. K. Brown Military Collection, Brown University)

to the ford of Faillie, four miles from the battlefield, under the guidance of Murray and the protection of Lord Ogilvy's two Angus Battalions which fought several rearguard actions against the Royal cavalry. From there they moved southwards into hilly country where it would be easier to avoid harassment.

On the moor, the guns fell silent for the first time in an hour. Now all that could be heard were the cries of the wounded in the heather, and the shouting and clatter of the Royal army as it prepared to advance. Shortly afterwards naval ships riding in the Moray Firth began to fire

salutes to the success of the army. Riding eastwards went one of Cumberland's aides, bound for Fort George and a Royal Navy ship which would carry the news of the victory to London. The Duke himself now moved forward through the front lines of his tired but jubilant troops, thanking each regiment for its efforts and ordering immediate refreshments to be handed out. In return he received loud 'huzzas' from his men, who shouted 'Billy! Billy!' and 'Flanders! Flanders!' The Duke then took up his position on the right and the order was given for a general advance, though the men of Barrell's and Munro's Regiments were allowed to stay where they were to tend their wounded. Marching the few hundred yards which had separated the two armies, the Royalists halted on the line where the Prince's regiments had deployed a few hours before. Again the troops cheered before sitting down to eat supplies brought up by the wagons. Having finished their brief repast, some of the soldiers rose and proceeded to bayonet any wounded Highlanders they could find. The Duke himself is said to have taken his lunch sitting on a stone at the eastern edge of the field. Although some of Cumberland's men were humane, there was a general tendency to show no mercy, especially in view of the captured note which, it was alleged, directed the Highland army to 'give no quarter, to the enemy'. Elsewhere on the field dragoons and foot were urged by General Hawley to kill any wounded Scotsmen. One English witness wrote: 'The moor was covered with blood and our men, what with killing the enemy, dabbling their feet in the blood, and splashing it about one another, looked like so many butchers rather than Christian soldiers.' A young wounded Highland officer gazed at Hawley who immediately ordered him to be killed. Legend has it that young James Wolfe, who was serving on Hawley's staff, refused to carry out the order and a soldier was found to do the job. Some of the Prince's commanders decided to place their fate in the hands of the enemy. Lord Balmerino, for one, refused Lord Elcho's plea to follow him off the field, and rode towards the enemy knowing full well the fate that awaited him. Lord Kilmarnock mistook some Royal dragoons for his own regiment and was immediately captured. Strathallan preferred to die rather than submit and, gathering some of his men around him, rode directly towards Cobham's dragoons, where he met his death by the sword of Colonel Howard.

After the battle Gillies MacBean had crawled to a wall six hundred yards from the field where several Royal troopers cut him down. In his last moments of life he dragged himself to a barn and died on the straw. Another Highlander tried in vain to keep the dragoons at bay with a pole from a wagon. John Fraser, an ensign in Lovat's Regiment, had been shot through the thigh and taken prisoner. He was taken to a nearby house

▲*James Wolfe (1727-59) had just turned 19 when Culloden was fought. The future conqueror of Quebec was a brigade-major in Barrel's Regiment, but he was with Hawley, serving as an aide when his Regiment was under attack. At the head of his company he would probably have been killed or wounded. His father's Regiment formed up en potence to Barrell's. The story that Wolfe was ordered by Cumberland to shoot a wounded Highlander, but the young man declined to do so is probably apocryphal. (Anne S. K. Brown Military Collection, Brown University)*

with other prisoners. Three days later they were taken to a field and shot. Fraser, though badly wounded and left for dead, managed to crawl to a nearby cottage where he recovered. Even innocent bystanders were not immune from the terror. Alexander Munro had gone to Drummossie to watch the battle but, given the confusion, decided to go to Inverness instead. On the way he and his companion were overtaken by dragoons. Munro ran into a field where he was cornered by a horseman whom he managed to bring down with a sword he had picked up near the battlefield.

The Royal army moved off in the direction of

▲'Prince Charles by the Nairn after Culloden', as depicted by Richard Beavis in 1878. Charles stated that he was 'forced off the field by the people around him' despite declaring that the enemy would not take him alive. Eventually persuaded to leave, he rode towards the ford of Faillie across the River Nairn accompanied by several officers before heading west, where he eluded the Royal troops for five months before fleeing to France. (Courtesy of the Omwell Gallery, London)

Inverness early in the afternoon. Along the road, a Jacobite drummer approached the Duke with an offer of surrender from General Stapleton who had commanded the Irish Picquets. Cumberland sent the messenger back with a letter assuring the General of fair treatment. The first infantry troops to enter the town were men from Sempill's Regiment under Captain Campbell who presented a strange appearance to the townspeople on account of the various assortment of hats and feathers removed from the Jacobite dead and now adorning the heads of the English soldiers. Shortly afterwards a group of dragoons entered the town with Cumberland as church bells rang and loud cheering filled the air. Loyalist prisoners, mostly Argyll Militiamen, were released from the prison and given a guinea each as compensation for their incarceration. Jacobite soldiers took their place. The last troops entered the town at about 4 o'clock. The wounded men, 259 in all, were given twelve guineas each from the Duke's own coffers while soldiers who had captured enemy standards received sixteen guineas. Tired from his bloody work, the Duke sought lodging in the home of Lady Macintosh, where two nights previously Prince Charles had stayed. Less than six miles away the wounded and dying clansmen lay on the soaking wet moor unattended by the Royal army surgeons who believed that English wounded had been neglected by the Jacobites at Prestonpans. Three ladies from Inverness ventured out to tend the wounded.

▶'Culloden Atrocities', as represented in a nineteenth-century lithograph. Had Cumberland contented himself with his victory he might have been remembered as a great soldier and leader of men, but his encouragement of the brutality and atrocities against the civilian population in Scotland branded him a 'Butcher' in the collective memory of the Highlands. (Anne S. K. Brown Military Collection, Brown University)

# THE AFTERMATH OF THE BATTLE

On the morning of Thursday 17 April, the dead soldiers of the Royal army were buried within an enclosure on Drummossie Moor. The army that had crossed the Spey had numbered approximately 8,811 men, of whom 6,411 were infantrymen. Casualties were given as 50 dead and 259 wounded. Of the officers, Lord Robert Kerr had been killed; Colonel Rich, who had commanded Barrell's, had lost a hand and was badly cut about the head, and a number of captains and lieutenants had been wounded. The brunt of the casualties were borne by the 438 men of Barrell's Regiment, seventeen of whom were killed and 108 wounded. In contrast, two regiments from the first line, two from the second line and one from reserve, together with the main group of Campbells, never fired a shot. It has been said that of the 14,000 belligerents at Culloden, possibly fewer than 3,000 men actually fought, the others either not having been called upon, as was the case of these English regiments, or fleeing the field, as many Highlanders did.

While the burial parties dug into the soggy ground they were aware of numerous wounded Highlanders still on the moor and as many as could be found were hastily dispatched. Drummossie and the surrounding fields and roads were strewn with Jacobite dead and although a count was made of the bodies, the government estimates may have been inaccurate; many of the wounded managed to hide from the Redcoats or died in cottages or barns. On the Friday after the battle, many were rounded up and executed by firing-squad. Cumberland ordered that all cottages in the neighbourhood of Culloden be searched for rebels: 'The officers and men will take notice that the Public orders of the rebels yesterday was to give us no quarter,' a claim which had no foundation. Of approximately 6,000 clansmen present with Prince Charles on 16 April, 2,000 may have become casualties. Some 336 Jacobites and 222 French were taken to Inverness and incarcerated in the gaol and in cellars of houses. More prisoners, mostly deserters from the Duke's

◀ *In this Victorian illustration by R. R. McIan, the artist has depicted a Jacobite fugitive of the Mackenzie clan still wearing in his bonnet the white cockade of the Stewarts and the badge of his clan, the wearing of which was punishable by transportation to the colonies. (Anne S. K. Brown Military Collection, Brown University)*

▶ *'After Culloden: Rebel Hunting', by John Seymour Lucas, painted in 1884 and representing a party of Cumberland's soldiers entering a blacksmith's shop in search of a rebel. The search for fugitives was conducted rigorously and many people were arrested merely for being Scottish. (Anne S. K. Brown Military Collection, Brown University)*

army were hanged from hastily erected gallows.

In Inverness, the Duke awoke early on the Thursday morning invigorated from the previous day's work. His task now was to prepare plans for the policing of the Highlands and the elimination of Jacobitism. 'All the good we have done is a little blood-letting, which has only weakened the madness, not cured it. I tremble for fear that this vile spot may still be the ruin of this island and our family,' he wrote. He was to spend the next three months in the town, directing his soldiers in their dirty work. Likewise, General Hawley was busy issuing orders for the extermination of the wounded Highlanders out on the moor.

Several miles away, the defeated Jacobite troops continued their withdrawal into the hills. There were still about 2,000 men under arms and they could have waged a guerrilla war, but no leader could be found. Charles had spent the evening after the battle at Gorthlick, fifteen miles from Culloden, but was preparing to rendezvous with a number of his soldiers at Fort Augustus. The majority of the fugitives, with Lord George Murray, Drummond, Perth and other leading

Jacobite officers, had gone in the direction of Ruthven, however, believing this to be the rallying place. And so Charles, cut off from the main Jacobite force, moved off westwards towards the coast, leaving a last brief command for his supporters: 'Let every man seek his own safety the best way he can.' At Ruthven, the Highlanders simply dispersed and went their own way, Murray penning a somewhat critical note to the Prince suggesting that the cause had been plagued from the beginning and that had the right field of battle been chosen and adequate supplies been to hand, the vanquished might have been the victors. Several weeks passed before Charles received the letter and from that time onwards he never forgave Murray.

As Charles Stuart headed for the Outer Hebrides, a number of his supporters, Lochiel in particular, still had ambitions to resist the enemy from the hills and a gathering was planned near Loch Arkaig, but less than six hundred men showed up. Ironically, two French privateers, *Mars* and *Bellona*, loaded with money to support the Rebellion, managed to reach the Scottish islands, having eluded three Royal Naval vessels. When they returned to France their passengers included several leading Jacobites, but Murray was not among them. He had set off towards the east coast but fell into the hands of Cumberland's dragoons at Polmood in the borders. After years of imprisonment in England he was released, having shifted his allegiance to the Hanoverians. He spent the last thirty years of his life in Hertfordshire.

On 20 April the Prince and several close associates including O'Sullivan reached Arisaig, almost nine months after putting ashore on that fateful July day. After spending a few days on the coast he gave his final address to his supporters before leaving in a small boat on the 26th. They landed on the small island of Benbecula in the Outer Hebrides, and word of his arrival quickly spread throughout the small communities. Royal ships and troops were combing the islands, so the Prince set off again towards Scalpay between Harris and Lewis, and then on to Stornoway. Thereafter he was constantly on the move al-

though he did spend three weeks at Corradale on South Uist. On 13 June he found himself within two miles of Cumberland's soldiers, and he was again forced to put to sea at Loch Boisdale. It was during this erratic itinerary that Charles was assisted by Flora Macdonald whom he had met at Milton on South Uist, and it was she who accompanied him to Skye, with the Prince disguised as a woman. The price on the Prince's head was tempting to many local lairds in the islands, and one in particular, Sir Alexander Macdonald, planned to betray him but was thwarted by the Prince's departure for Skye. Flora Macdonald was later arrested in Skye and imprisoned but released the following year. Charles sailed to the island of Raasay on 1 July and eventually made his way back to the mainland, constantly moving to avoid capture. Eventually, on 19 September, he and his colleagues reached Borrodale where two small French vessels were ready to take them to France and exile. In 1788, drunken and disillusioned, the Prince died in Rome.

During Cumberland's stay in Inverness the Royal troops penetrated deeper into the Highlands in their search for the Prince. The Duke moved to Fort Augustus with the bulk of his army leaving four battalions at Inverness to guard the north. Three infantry battalions held the rebels in check in Perthshire and Aberdeenshire, and the west was

policed by a large garrison at Fort William. In Argyllshire, 2,000 loyalist Campbells ruthlessly stamped out pockets of Jacobite resistance. There were many atrocious incidents although once in a while it was the Royal troops who were the victims. Behind the barracks at Fort Augustus, the bodies of nine soldiers were found, which spurred the Royal troops to ever worse reprisals.

When Cumberland returned to London he was treated as a hero, receiving honours and money and being lionized by society. The cheering of the throngs who came to welcome the 'conquering hero' must have been heard by the Jacobite prisoners held in the Tower. In all, 3,470 had been taken into custody, some just for wishing the Highlanders success. The executions on Tower Hill followed soon, including those of Kilmarnock and Balmerino who were beheaded. Others were hanged, drawn and quartered. A fate (some said) worse than death – transportation to the colonies to be sold – awaited 936 Scotsmen. Some were banished, others simply disappeared, their fate unknown. In Scotland, the Disarming Acts brought a brief end to the wearing of Highland dress and the use of bagpipes. Clan chiefs were reduced by other acts to becoming ordinary landlords, overseeing remote and desolate moorlands. In short the Scottish way of life was eliminated, but it gradually re-emerged in the late

◀'End of the '45', by W. B. Hole, a Victorian representation. Culloden was not only the end of a failed rebellion, but signalled the end of a way of life for thousands in the Scottish Highlands. Whole communities were uprooted as the men were rounded up and imprisoned or transported to the colonies. (Anne S. K. Brown Military Collection, Brown University)

# Aftermath: The Flight of the Pretender

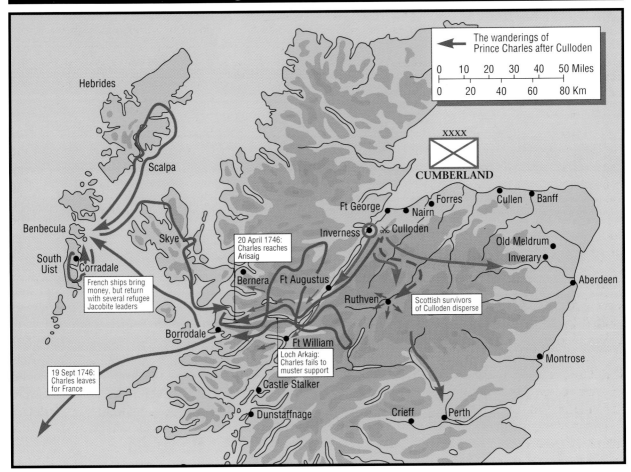

eighteenth century although in a modified form. 'Butcher' Cumberland did not live to see the brief renaissance of Scottish culture; he died on 31 October 1765. His crowning glory had been Culloden, but he was never forgiven for the crimes committed in his name after the battle.

The outcome of Culloden might have been much different had Charles paid heed to his advisers, in particular Murray, and not to the hot-headed O'Sullivan. The Prince was an indifferent commander and the odds were against him before the first shot had been fired. Had the battle been fought at the site suggested by Murray on 17 April, who knows what might have happened? But in his stubbornness lay the seeds of his own destruction. His obsession with the notion that to retreat from one's enemy was unchivalrous doomed his army to fight on ground that favoured the enemy. If the

walls of Culloden Park been knocked down the major threat to the Jacobite wings would have been eliminated. O'Sullivan felt that the removal of the walls would have distorted the Jacobite lines, but in fact the walls served to immobilize large elements of the Highland army. A bad situation was exacerbated by the abysmal standard of communications between the Jacobite regiments. It was stated that the Prince sent the order to attack eight times to Murray before the order was acted upon.

To this day, the name Culloden conjures varying emotions in Britain. The Scottish nation has never forgotten the dreadful aftermath of the battle, which is recalled in numerous ballads. Books and films have added to the mystique, but the barbarism to which the Scots were subjected after the battle left a permanent stain on the British

Army and no regiment has ever claimed the right to the battle honour, preferring instead to play down their role in the business. It was the last battle fought by armies on British soil and one which created a lasting ill-will between the two nations which even today emerges from time to time.

◄'Simon Fraser, Lord Lovat'(1667-1747), by Hogarth, painted at St. Albans after Lovat's arrest. He was one of the first to invite the Pretender to Scotland in 1737, but it was not until the victory at Prestonpans that Lovat threw his support behind the cause. He was arrested, but escaped from Inverness. His son fought in the battle but Lovat himself stayed at home. After the débâcle he tried unsuccessfully to persuade Charles to make one last stand. Lovat fled the scene but was arrested and taken to the Tower where he was beheaded. (Anne S. K. Brown Military Collection, Brown University)

▼Execution of the rebel lords as depicted in a contemporary engraving published in August 1746. The reprisals against former Jacobites and their sympathizers were excessive. On 29 May 1746 the Earl of Kilmarnock, Lord Balmarino and the Earl of Cromarty were brought to the Tower of London, where a grand jury sentenced them to death. Kilmarnock and Balmerino were beheaded on Great Tower Hill on 18 August. (Anne S. K. Brown Military Collection)

# THE BATTLEFIELD TODAY

Even at the time Culloden was recognised as having been an extremely significant event in Scottish history, and the battlefield has attracted a constant stream of visitors ever since. Unlike all-too many British sites it remains largely unspoilt and has much to offer both casual visitors and serious students of military history.

In the 18th century the area was not covered in heather, but was instead a broad area of common grazing land chiefly used by the tenants of the adjacent Culloden estate, and so called in order to distinguish it from the much larger Drummossie Moor of which it forms a part. It lies some 5 miles outside Inverness and is best approached along the B9006 road from that city – or directly from the A9 trunk road. There is also an alternative approach available from the A92 Aberdeen-Inverness road. Both routes are well signposted, and although most visitors will arrive by car or coach, a bracing walk up the road from Inverness is recommended if time allows – the return journey is downhill. One of the attractions of walking this route is that the same road was used by Jacobite troops marching to the battlefield – and running away from it afterwards.

The site itself has a large, well appointed, visitor centre and car-park run by the National Trust for Scotland (NTS), situated at Old Leanach in an area which was occupied during the battle by the left of the British Army's second line. The visitor centre has a good cafe, toilets and well-stocked bookshop to which entry is free. Payment of the usual fee secures admission both to a museum and interpretative area and to the adjacent Old Leanach farmhouse itself. Once thought to have been standing at the time of the battle, recent research has revealed that the existing building was actually built in about 1760. It does, however, stand on the site of an earlier steading. According to tradition an adjacent barn full of Jacobite wounded was burned by Cumberland's troops after the battle, but in all likelihood it was actually used at the time as a British Army field hospital.

The National Trust for Scotland also currently owns about a third of the battlefield. A forestry plantation, which obscured much of the Trust's landholding for many years, has been cleared, but secondary growth is unchecked at the time of writing. The old Inverness road that slashed across the moor in 1746 has also been diverted to carry modern traffic around the north of the Trust land, but its original course can still be traced quite easily.

A number of grave markers were erected in 1881 and a number of other stones and memorials are traditionally, if sometimes dubiously, associated with various individuals and units. More recently a network of paths and markers have been set out by the Trust with the intention of leading visitors to the original positions occupied by the regiments which fought there. Current research, however, suggests that they are wrongly placed and generally set too closely together.

There are no doubts, on the other hand, as to the scene of the fiercest fighting, which is easily identified by a large oval cluster of mass graves placed on either side of what was the old road. It was here that the Jacobite right wing overran Barrell's 4th Foot, only to be cut down in a murderous cross-fire at point-blank range when Major General Huske counter-attacked through the Old Leanach steading area. It is all-too easy to stand there now amongst the long low mounds and get a feel for what happened on that spot in April 1746.

Just to the south of this area the National Trust for Scotland have recently uncovered the foundations of the turf-walled Leanach enclosure and dry-stone walled Culwhiniac enclosure, which funnelled the charging Jacobites towards Barrell's Regiment, and both have been partially reconstructed.

Further back still is the now disused steading at Culchunaig, which marked the Jacobite left flank at the outset of the fighting. The present buildings considerably post-date the battle, but it is well worth walking down the track from the farm building towards the B851 road. On one side of the track are the remains of the original dry-stone wall breached by the Argyle Militia during the battle, and on the other side is a small stream set in a prominent re-entrant stretching back to another steading at Balvraid, well in the Jacobite rear. Having passed through the breaches torn in the wall Hawley's dragoons formed up along the southern edge of the re-entrant, but were initially prevented from crossing by a substantial force of Jacobite cavalry and infantry posted on the crest above. The re-entrant is easily found but it lies on private land and visitors should behave appropriately.

All in all, it is recommended that serious visitors should arm themselves with an up-to-date 1:25000 scale map of the area, and a copy of Thomas Sandby's well-known contemporary one (See *Like Hungry Wolves* pages 80-81). The tour should then be conducted around the contemporary landmarks such as the Old Leanach steading and enclosure, the upper and lower Culwhiniac enclosures (still easily identifiable),

Culchunaig, and the long re-entrant which was the scene of Hawley's virtually separate battle, and above all that long slew of mass graves close by the aptly-named "Well of the Dead", where the last Jacobite charge was shot down in bloody ruin.

A whole day should be allowed for the visit if it is intended to walk out from Inverness, and as most of the moor is still just as boggy as it was in 1746; a stout pair of boots and gaiters is essential if it is intended to stray off the official paths. Otherwise the site can be comfortably viewed in a couple of hours, leaving ample time for a subsidiary visit to the magnificent Fort George at nearby Ardersier. Other local sites worthy of attention include the Civil War battlefield of Auldearn, just outside Nairn (Hawley's cavalry were quartered there on the night before the battle), and Ruthven Barracks, which overlook the A9 near Kingussie.

(Stuart Reid Author of *Like Hungry Wolves*, Windrow & Greene, 1994)

# GUIDE TO FURTHER READING

Some forty years after its publication, the extensive account of the Battle of Culloden, John Prebble's *Culloden*, London, 1961 is still an important and extensive work as is. Stuart Reid's *Like Hungry Wolves* London, 1994. A year after Prebble's book appeared, an excellent study of the battles and the background to the Jacobite rebellion of 1745 appeared: Tomasson, K. and Buist, F. *Battles of The '45*, London 1962. The campaign in England following Prestonpans and preceding Falkirk has been fully described in Frank McLynn's *The Jacobite Army in England 1745*, Edinburgh, 1983.

For biographical details of the opposing commanders see: Speck, W. A. *The Butcher*, Oxford 1981; and Charteris, Hon. E. *William Augustus, Duke of Cumberland*, London 1913. For Charles Edward Stuart see Maclean, Fitzroy, *Bonnie Prince*

*Charlie*, London 1988; and McLynn, Frank, *Charles Edward Stuart: A Tragedy in Many Acts*, London 1988.

In terms of the opposing armies, McLynn's study contains also the best account of the organization and composition of the Jacobite army. One of the best studies of the British army of the eighteenth century is Houlding, J. A., *Fit for Service. The Training of the British Army, 1715–1795*, Oxford 1981. Other useful studies include: Tomasson, K., *The Jacobite General*, Edinburgh and London, 1958.

Two of the best contemporary accounts written by combatants are: Johnstone, the Chevalier de, *A Memoir of the 'Forty-Five*, London, 1958; and Elcho, David, Lord, *A Short Account of the Affairs of Scotland in the Years 1744, 1745, and 1746*, Edinburgh, 1907.

# CHRONOLOGY

**Events leading up to the Battle of Culloden**
**16 July 1745** Charles Edward Stuart sets sail from France.
**25 July** The French ships *Du Teillay* and *Elizabeth* anchor off the Scottish mainland near Arisaig.
**3 August** Charles lands in Scotland.
**19 August** Charles raises the Stuart Royal Standard at Glenfinnan.
**17 September** The Prince enters Edinburgh.
**21 September** The Battle of Prestonpans – defeat of Cope.
**21 September to 1 November** Jacobite army in Edinburgh.
**8 November** Invasion of England.
**5 December** The Prince at Derby – decision to retreat.
**20 December** Jacobites cross back into Scotland.
**17 January 1746** The Battle of Falkirk – defeat of Hawley.
**30 January** Cumberland arrives at Leith.
**1 February** Jacobites retreat into the Highlands.
**Mid-February to mid-April** Charles at Inverness.
**8 April** The Royal army leaves Aberdeen.
**11 April** Cumberland reaches Cullen.
**14 April** The Royal army crosses the River Spey.
**14 April** Jacobite army quits Inverness for Culloden.
**15 April** Jacobites fail to surprise Royal army.
**16 April Battle of Culloden**:
   **4 a.m.** Reveille in the Government camp.

**5 a.m.** Cumberland's army commences march to field.
**6 a.m.** Main part of Jacobite army returns to Culloden.
**7 a.m.** The Prince returns from Inverness.
**11 a.m.** Two sides come into view.
**1 p.m.** Opposing armies in position.
***c*.1.05 p.m.** Jacobite artillery opens fire.
***c*.1.08 p.m.** Government artillery open fire.
***c*.1.08 p.m.** Argyll Militia move towards enclosures on left wing.
**1.30 p.m.** Order to advance given by Jacobites.
***c*.1.35 p.m.** Jacobite right wing crashes into left of Government line.
***c*.1.40 p.m.** Royal Artillery ceases fire.
***c*.1.50 p.m.** Retreat of Jacobites.
***c*.1.50 p.m.** Flanking movements by Government dragoons.
***c*.2 p.m.** Advance of the Royal army across moor.
***c*.2.30 p.m.** Government troops march off towards Inverness.
**4 p.m.** Last Government troops enter Inverness.

**Events following the Battle of Culloden**
**17 April** Burial of Government dead at Culloden.
**20 April to 18 September** Charles's movements in the Hebrides.
**19 September** Charles disembarks for France.
**30 September** Arrives off Roscoff, France.

# GLOSSARY

**bayonet** A dagger-like weapon fixing near the muzzle of a rifle or bayonet. (p.27 fig. 3, 29, 44)

**bore** The diameter of a gun barrel. Sometimes expressed as the number of musket bullets of the correct size that could be made from a pound of lead; e.g. 12 bore. (p.29)

**broadsword** Smaller weapon adopted in place of the two-handed claymore. (p.34, 36, 38 fig.2)

**canister** An artillery missile consisting of metal fragments in a canister. (p.33)

**cartridge** A tube containing powder and a bullet for a musket. (p.29)

**claymore** "Claidheamh mor", a large, two-handed sword. Also the order to charge. (p.40, 55)

**grape** Grape shot, an artillery weapon consisting of many musket balls, like a shot gun. (p.60)

**grenade or grenado** An explosive missile thrown by a grenadier. (p.33)

**halberd** A weapon consisiting of a blade mounted on a staff. (p.30)

**hanger** A light, one-edged sword. (p.29)

**paillass** A straw-filled mattress. (p.28)

**plaid** A large (6 feet by 18 feet or 1.8 metre by 5.5 metre) piece of tartan cloth used as a garment, the belted plaid. (p.34, 42, 53)

**spontoon** A half-pike, a short spear carried by an officer. (p.27 fig. 2)

**targe or target** A round shield. (p.34)

**trews** Close-fitting trousers. (p.38 fig. 1, 67)

# INDEX

# PLACES TO VISIT

## North-west Scotland

*The Battle of Glenshiel, 10 June 1719*
*Location: About five miles south-east of Shiel Bridge where the A87 crosses the River Shiel. A nearby cairn marks the old bridge. National Trust for Scotland information board.*

The 1,600 Highlanders were ranged up the hillside to the north of the road with 250 Spanish troops next to the river and Lord George Murray's men south of the river. The afternoon saw little action until 5pm when General Joseph Wightman's right climbed round the Highlanders' left. Murray's men fell back and the Jacobites swiftly collapsed, fleeing into the hills. The Spaniards, with no such option, surrendered.

*Bernera Barracks*
*Location: Eight miles west of Shiel Bridge via Glenelg.*

Bernera is one of four barracks built in the 1720s and it survives largely as it was. The Glenelg Brochs, stone towers, are nearby.

*Fort Augustus and Kiliwhimen Barracks*
*Location: The Benedictine Abbey and the Lovat Arms Hotel in Fort Augustus.*

Kiliwhimen was the largest of the barracks built after the failure of the 1715 uprising, housing six companies (360 men). General Wade declared himself dissatisfied with it in 1724 when it was scarcely finished; too small and too far from the loch itself. He built a new fortress close to the water, a square fort with huge corner bastions, only one of which survives at the Abbey. The barracks, too, have gone, leaving just one stretch of musket-looped wall behind the hotel.

*The Military Road*

The B862 to Whitebridge, along the south of Loch Ness, is a military road. A mile south of Fort Augustus, off the A82 to Fort William, is a minor road running south-east on the south-west side of Glen Tarff. This is one end of the military road over the Corrieyairack Pass, negotiable only on foot over the pass itself.

*Fort William*
*Location: In Fort William, behind the railway station on the north of the town and at Craigs Burial Ground.*

In 1689 a new fort was based on an older one, close to the River Nevis and Loch Linnhe. It was abandoned in 1864 and largely destroyed in 1889 to make way for the railway station. Parts of the north and west bastion, including the sallyport, are to be found behind the station and the burial ground boasts the old main gate as well as soldiers' headstones.

*The West Highland Museum*
*Location: Cameron Square, Fort William.*
*Tel: (01397) 702169*
Information on the fort and on the Jacobite risings.

*Glencoe*
*Location: Seventeen miles south of Fort William by A82. National Trust for Scotland Vistor Center.*
*Tel: (01855) 811307 (summer only).*

*Glenfinnan*
*Location: Eighteen miles west of Fort William by A830. National Trust for Scotland Monument (open site) and Visitor Centre, open April to October daily.*
*Tel: (01397) 722250.*
Here Prince Charles Edward, the Young Pretender, raised his standard on 19 August 1745. The story of the '45 rebellion is told in full at the Visitor Centre.

## North-east Scotland

*Fort George*
*Location: Four miles north of the A96 Inverness-Nairn road, via Ardersier. Historic Scotland. Open all year.*
*Tel: (01667) 462777.*

The original fort of this name was built on the site of Inverness Castle on which Cromwell had built a citadel. It was taken by the Jacobites in 1746 and blown up. A new fort was built some eleven miles north-east on the southern shore of the Moray Firth in 1747. The result is one of the finest, and largest, fortresses in Britain. Virtually unaltered to this day, it is a superb example of the 18th century artillery fort. Reconstructed barrack rooms portray the life of the Hanoverian soldier and the Seafield Collection of arms completes the picture.

*The Battle of Culloden Moor, 16 April 1746*
*Location: Five miles east of Inverness by B9006. National Trust for Scotland Visitor Centre, open daily all year.*
*Tel: (01463) 790607. Numerous landmarks and memorials also in the care of the Trust.*
See pages 89/90.

*Ruthven Barracks. Location: Kingussie. Historic Scotland.*
Ruthven in Badenoch was chosen as the site of one of the four barracks built in the aftermath of the 1715 uprising.

Completed in 1724, it consists of two blocks facing each other across a square secured at either end with walls with musket-loops and a walkway above, enough to resist lightly armed troops but not artillery, and with corner turrets to enfilade attacks.

### The Military Road
*Location: Laggan, eleven miles west of Kingussie by A86, and minor road straight on up the Spey valley.*
In 1727 General Wade proposed a road from Loch Ness to Ruthven over the Corrieyairack Pass. It may be traced past Garvamore Barracks west of Laggan by car, but only on foot all the way to Glen Tarff and Fort Augustus.

### The Skirmish at Inverurie, 23 December 1745
*Location: Twenty miles north-west of Aberdeen, the Bass of Inverurie, south of the town on B993, around the old churchyard.*
With the intention of taking Aberdeen from the Jacobites Macleod of Macleod led 700 men south from Inverness in mid-December 1745. They halted at Inverurie, uncertain as to the situation in Aberdeen, and during the delay the Jacobites organised an attack. A column under Gordon of Avochie moved up the main road while Lord Lewis Gordon took 900 men to the east. The Macleods had men around the churchyard and the Bass (the ruins of a motte and bailey castle) but the fords over the Don and the Urie were unguarded. In the late afternoon the Jacobites attacked from east and west, putting the Macleods to flight with ease.

### Braemar Castle
*Location: North of the A93 just east of Braemar.*
A tower house where the Earl of Mar raised his standard in 1715, it was forfeit on the failure of the rising. It was leased for 99 years for a rent of £14 a year to the Hanoverian government in 1748 and converted to a barracks for occupying troops. The star-shaped outer wall was also added. The castle secured part of the military road, now approximating to the A93, from Blairgowrie.

### Corgarff Castle
*Location: Fourteen miles north of Ballater on the A939 Grantown-on-Spey road. Historic Scotland.*
*Open daily in summer, weekends in winter.*
*Tel (opening times): (0131) 668 8800.*
The military road from Blairgowrie to Fort George, built between 1749 and 1754 and now approximating to the A93 and A939, swings up into the hills from Braemar - a route of vital strategic importance. Just to the south of the castle a length of it can be walked and north of it, on the A939, is a memorial to its builders. The 16th century tower house at Corgarff, which had been used by the Jacobites in both the '15 and the '45, was converted to a fortified barracks by 1750.

### The Battle of Killiekrankie, 27 July 1689
*Location: National Trust for Scotland Visitor Centre, three miles north of Pitlochry by B8079. Open April to October.*
*Tel: (01796) 473233. Battlesite open all year.*

General Hugh Mackay had reached Urrard House by the afternoon of 27 July when Viscount Dundee's Jacobite army was seen coming over the high ground above the road. Their forces were hastily drawn up above the River Garry, but for two hours little took place; Mackay could not launch an attack uphill and Dundee's men had the sun in their eyes. As dusk fell the Highlanders charged the over-extended government lines and swept them away, though "Bonnie Dundee" died in the hour of victory.

## Central Scotland

### The Battle of Sheriffmuir, 13 November 1715
*Location: East of Dunblane (5 miles north of Stirling), on the minor road to Blackford via Pisgah. The Macrae Monument is where road kinks right and is joined by path from Dunblane.*
The Earl of Mar raised his standard at Braemar on 6 September 1715. The Duke of Argyll moved the small government force of some 3,000 men to Stirling to prevent Mar's 7,000 moving into the south from Perth. On the morning of 13 November they faced each other across the moorland near Dumblane, about a mile and a half apart, probably on either side of the site of the Macrae Monument, Argyll's men with their backs towards Dunblane. Their fronts overlapped; Argyll's right outflanking Mar's left, and Mar's right Argyll's left. The Scottish charge was held and repulsed by Argyll's right while his left was scattered and chased as far as Stirling. The battle front turned anti-clockwise and Mar's main body of troops were pushed back over the river at Kinbuck to the north-west. While neither side could claim a decisive victory on the field, the Jacobite cause received a fatal setback.

### The Battle of Falkirk, 17 January 1746
*Location: South of Falkirk by B803, past junction with B8023, bear right opposite hospital and right to Bantaskin Park; monument and the ravine. Also, continue past hospital on B803, stop short of sharp left turn and look back from position of Jacobite right.*
See pages 17/20.

### The Battle of Prestonpans, 21 September 1745
*Location: North of Tranent (10 miles east of Edinburgh) on the B6371, north of the junction with the A198.*
The site is built over to some extent and the A1 cuts across the line of the Jacobite move around the east of Cope's positions. The first and second positions of the English had the modern location of Preston railway station at the south or west and the third was facing east across the road, now the B6371, which still follows the same line. The Jacobite approach was south of the modern A1 by a minor road from the west to take position astride the B6414 and south of the line of the old A1 which went through Tranent itself. See pages 12/15.

# England

*Carlisle Castle*
*Location: Castle Way, Carlisle. English Heritage.*
*Tel: (01228) 591922. Open April to October daily 9.30am*
*to 6pm, November to March 10am to 4pm.*
An exhibition devoted to the Jacobite risings can be seen here. See Page 15.

*The Battle of Clifton Moor, 18 December 1745*
*Location: Clifton, two miles south of Penrith by A6.*
As Lord George Murray, the Jacobite commander, reached Clifton he learned that the Hanoverians were close behind and observed men appearing to the south, drawn up in two lines. They were Bland's Regiment, Kerr's Dragoons and part of Ligonier's Horse. The Duke of Perth made for Penrith to seek reinforcements while, in the setting sun, Murray deployed his troops just south of the village, from right to left, Glengarry men, Col Roy Stewart's, Stewarts of Appin and Cluny's Macphersons, about 1,000 men in all. The trap was set with the Gelgarry men concealed on the west behind a stone wall, ready to fire, Roy Stewart on the edge of the village near the church and the rest along the hedges and embankments of the lane heading south-east to Cliburn. No reinforcements arrived.

Some 500 dragoon's advanced dismounted, cautiously working through the little enclosures. In the fitful moonlight they could see little of the Scots, but were themselves easy to see. Murray ordered Cluny forward to a hedge running north/south which turned out to be lined with dragoons and concealed a ditch. There was an exchange of fire, followed by a charge to Murray's cry of "Claymore!" The dragoons were thrown back into the flanking fire of the Glengarrys and tried no more. Under the cover of darkness the Jacobites withdrew safely to Penrith. The last battle on English soil had left something above two dozen dead. A monument to Bland's Regiment stands in the churchyard. See page 17.

## Traveller's References

Marix Evans, Martin, *The Military Heritage of Britain and Ireland*, London, André Deutsch, 1998

Seymour, William, *Battles in Britain 1066 - 1746*, Ware, Wordsworth Editions, 1997

Smurthwaite, David, *The Complete Guide to the Battlefields of Britain*, London, Michael Joseph, 1993

Tabaham, Chris and Doreen Grove, *Fortress Scotland and the Jacobites*, London, B. T. Batsford / Historic Scotland, 1996

---

## COMPANION SERIES FROM OSPREY

**MEN-AT-ARMS**
An unrivalled source of information on the organisation, uniforms and equipment of the world's fighting men, past and present. The series covers hundreds of subjects spanning 5,000 years of history. Each 48-page book includes concise texts packed with specific information, some 40 photos, maps and diagrams, and eight colour plates of uniformed figures.

**ELITE**
Detailed information on the uniforms and insignia of the world's most famous military forces. Each 64-page book contains some 50 photographs and diagrams, and 12 pages of full-colour artwork.

**NEW VANGUARD**
Comprehensive histories of the design, development and operational use of the world's armoured vehicles and artillery. Each 48-page book contains eight pages of full-colour artwork including a detailed cutaway.

**WARRIOR**
Definitive analysis of the armour, weapons, tactics and motivation of the fighting men of history. Each 64-page book contains cutaways and exploded artwork of the warrior's weapons and armour.

**ORDER OF BATTLE**
The most detailed information ever published on the units which fought history's great battles. Each 96-page book contains comprehensive organisation diagrams supported by ultra-detailed colour maps. Each title also includes a large fold-out base map.

**AIRCRAFT OF THE ACES**
Focuses exclusively on the elite pilots of major air campaigns, and includes unique interviews with surviving aces sourced specifically for each volume. Each 96-page volume contains up to 40 specially commissioned artworks, unit listings, new scale plans and the best archival photography available.

**COMBAT AIRCRAFT**
Technical information from the world's leading aviation writers on the aircraft types flown. Each 96-page volume contains up to 40 specially commissioned artworks, unit listings, new scale plans and the best archival photography available.